modern
vintage style

RYLAND
PETERS
& SMALL

LONDON NEW YORK

modern vintage style

Emily Chalmers
Words by Ali Hanan

Photography by Debi Treloar

Senior designer Megan Smith
Editor Rebecca Woods
Location research Jess Walton
Head of production Patricia
Harrington
Art director Leslie Harrington
Publishing director Alison Starling

First published in 2011 by
Ryland Peters & Small
20–21 Jockey's Fields
London WC1R 4BW
and
519 Broadway, 5th Floor
New York, NY 10012
www.rylandpeters.com

10 9 8 7 6 5 4 3 2 1

Text © Emily Chalmers 2011
Design and photographs
© Ryland Peters & Small 2011

ISBN: 978-1-84975-099-8

A CIP record for this book is
available from the British Library.

Printed and bound in China

Library of Congress Cataloging-in-
Publication Data:

Chalmers, Emily.
  Modern vintage style / Emily
Chalmers ; words by Ali Hanan ;
photography by Debi Treloar. -- 1st
US ed.
      p. cm.
  Includes index.
  ISBN 978-1-84975-099-8
  1. Antiques in interior decoration.
I. Hanan, Ali. II. Treloar, Debi. III. Title.
  NK2115.5.A5C49 2011
  747--dc22
                        2010049036

For digital editions visit
rylandpeters.com/apps.php

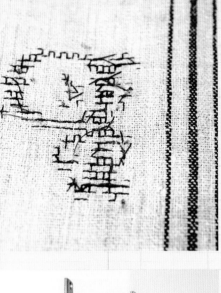

contents

introduction

Modern Vintage Style is no ordinary 'style' book. As you'll see throughout these pages, 'modern vintage' goes beyond being a 'look'. For many of these homeowners and the book's creators – stylist Emily Chalmers, purveyor of boutique shop Caravan and photographer Debi Treloar – 'modern vintage' is a passion. They're always on the look out for unusual, quirky, inventive pieces to restore, reinvent and rescue. The interiors in this book are not just inspiring homes, but are also a reflection of some rather extraordinary people.

Every homeowner here cherry-picks the best of the old, the crème of the new and then adds their own flair. Nottingham homeowners Tim Rundle and his partner Glynn Jones collect kitsch souvenirs, retro lights and Roman busts; Norfolk textile artist Petra Boase cloaks her walls in stripes of vintage wallpaper; French artist Claire Basler inhabits a meadow-like interior filled with enormous blooms. All these homeowners have traits in common: they're resourceful, creative and inventive.

For the modern vintage look doesn't come from a catalogue. Without a little vintage, sleek, modern interiors can seem soulless. And, without a modern context, vintage pieces seem fusty and staid. Yet, when they come together, interiors become completely fresh.

The style also feels right for now, tapping into the zeitgeist for reusing, recycling and re-purposing. More than ever, we're conscious that instead of constantly buying new things, we must look after and recycle the old.

Besides being kinder to the environment, pieces of yesteryear are made with care and craftsmanship. Rebelling against an age of cheap mass production, we now revere the art of the handmade, the errant line of a hand-stitch, the thick daub of paint on a wall mural or the painstaking patience of the embroiderer.

Recently, there has been a revival in home 'arts', and many of us are rejuvenating old skills: knitting our bedspreads, stitching our own cushions, even crafting toys or rescuing old ones. Use for inspiration the homes of craft artist, Nathalie Lete, who reincarnates old soft toys, or French textile artist Aurelie Mathigot, who has knitted, customized or crocheted almost everything in her home.

Vintage furniture pieces are also an ode to great quality. Once designed to last for life, they were made of fine, sturdy materials: beds were forged from intricately-wrought iron, sofas covered with resilient leathers and hand-woven linens were passed down from generation to generation. Source pieces like these and they will last you a lifetime, too.

The style won't break your budget. Many vintage pieces cost next to nothing, like the stunning lamp in Nadia Yaron and Myriah Scruggs' Brooklyn bathroom, found on Craig's List for just US$35. Other previously neglected but now-loved pieces were unearthed in flea markets, jumble sales, car boot sales, second-hand shops or church fairs. When you find them, it's like winning the style lottery.

And, for some of these owners, their passion has become their day-to-day business. Hannah Plumb and James Russell recycle other people's hand-me-downs to produce elegant interiors. Yaron and Scruggs, work together

plucking found wood off the street; they then
fashion pieces into furniture, softening them
with discarded fabrics. They'll often go on
hunts, foraging at night for pieces to reuse
in interesting ways and sell them on.

Others are just passionate about great
design. For Rundle and Jones, they simply love
collecting, bringing home things from their
travels that become part of their home's DNA.
Their finds are from a huge array of sources,
including Italian markets, eBay, tacky souvenir
shops and even a Chinese take-away. Their
home is a constant work in progress.

Yet, like many of the owners here, they'll
also combine their pieces with high street buys,
sourcing pieces from Habitat and IKEA. While
vintage has its many advantages, many high
street shops champion new designers, and
have chic retro reproduction pieces that look
just right beside their vintage counterparts.

These interiors look eclectic, yet overall
themes make the style work in harmony. Your
space needs to look artfully edited; you don't
want a room cluttered with an odd assortment
of décor that doesn't hang together. Modern
vintage works through a rhythm of unexpected
pairings. When you choose something vintage,
make sure something modern is not far away.

Otherwise, find a 'red thread' of colour.
In Ann Shore's London kitchen, she's kept to
a palette of fresh blue and crisp white, while
Petra Boase chooses a Fifties palette of pastel
shades. Pick modern and vintage pieces and
underpin them with a colour theme.

Transitional pieces that straddle both
modern and vintage eras also act as unifying
elements, tying the style together. One or two
timeless classics, like reproductions of Charles
Eames' loungers or Mies van der Rohe's

Barcelona day beds, bring together the old and
the new. Sometimes, choosing styles that share
a design ethic also brings visual harmony.
Mid-century modern somehow connects with
minimalist Japanese, while modern country
furniture sits well with antique examples.

Whatever you do, enjoy the journey. None
of these homes have been created overnight.
They've been a labour of love. These homeowners have let their interiors unfold around
their passions, embracing the kitsch, the
quirky and the eccentric. Be inspired to create
your own home of modern vintage and you, too,
will be truly passionate about the place you live.

inspiration

furniture

Every piece you'll buy for your modern vintage home will come with a story. Pieces will land from many places: from far-off lands, junk shops or a lucky find on the internet. You'll inherit bits and bobs from grandparents and uncover lost pieces on street corners. In many cases, they may need a repair and a lick of paint or varnish, but if the bones are solid, then these pieces are raw treasures, just awaiting your tender loving care.

When it comes to furniture, remember that in modern vintage style, opposites attract. Nothing has to match. Your own taste will bind it all together. Pieces will contrast and combine in harmonious fashion if everything is chosen with your style in mind. Trust your own instincts. And whatever you know about the 'rules', discard them all.

Except one. Think contrast. When pieces clash you highlight their features, so juxtapose different styles and eras in your arrangement. When you choose a modern piece, think vintage; whenever you're going too traditional, it's time to inject a touch of the contemporary. That way you strike a balance.

If you like a piece, but it's not quite right, consider style surgery. Take a fusty floral seat cover and replace it with one in a bold colour or with thick stripes. An item with chipped paint, worn corners or an outdated colour can be easily reinvented in an afternoon with a coat of brightly coloured paint. And, simply pairing dark, heavy vintage pieces with chrome or galvanized metal, adds a touch of urban cool, loft style.

Some furniture needs space to breathe. Modern design means clean surfaces with small pockets of display. So if you find a vintage roll-top desk or an exquisite Chinese wardrobe, let it stand alone in the limelight instead of cluttering it with accessories. Otherwise, just put one equally beautiful piece on its horizontal top.

Striking pieces can become sculptures in themselves. Site them in redundant corners, like stair landings or hallways. Ornamental chairs, Victorian trestle tables, old sewing machines or Far Eastern-style dressing tables can all become more than just furniture, but also beautiful, alluring pieces. Make people stop and stare at these *objets d'art*.

Let's look at key pieces of furniture in each room. The living room, probably your most multi-functional space, seems a good place to start. Here, the sofa rules. These kings of the living room have been subject to trends throughout history, depending on the attitudes of the era, from the elegant three-way Victorian conversation chair to the Seventies-style low-level 'conversation pit' sofa. Mid-century modern sofas, like those created by Charles and Ray Eames and Mies van der Rohe, were based on the principle that form and function are inextricably linked. With simple, clean lines, they demanded no unnecessary ornamentation. If you find one of these pieces, juxtapose it with traditional furniture, such as old tea chests or high-back wooden chairs.

Old Chesterfield sofas, with tufting and decorative buttons, are timeless classics. With large, rolled arms and built-in cushions, they traditionally came in leather and velvets, but you can always take the shape and give it your own modern twist, perhaps covering the seat with a thick piece of hemp. Other classics include Chippendale sofas, which have an

reinvent, rediscover Some of the best pieces of furniture are ones you'll find or inherit. Old filing drawers (*above*) still have the alphabet embossed on their fronts, yet in their new life they make stylish storage. Brooklyn homeowners and up-cyclers Nadia Yaron and Myriah Scruggs have created a whole business from finding old pieces of furniture or fashioning pieces from found wood and recycled fabrics, like this old hipster (*opposite*).

idiosyncratic camel-back shape and a singular uninterrupted seat cushion. Harking back to the 19th century, you can easily bring one of these sofas up to date by covering the long cushion in a fabric of a more recent vintage. Lastly, there's the 'fainting couch' or the chaise longue. In the 19th century, women's corsets were so tight that it was not uncommon to faint after climbing the stairs, hence the nickname. Reupholster these sofas and give them a luxe make-over with zebra prints, colourful velvets or bright, graphic fabrics.

Conversely, if you own a modern high street sofa, it's easy to give it an injection of vintage with a Sixties graphic throw, a piece of old lace, a montage of cushions or a crocheted blanket.

Combine the rest of your living room furniture around this one key piece. Select contrasting armchairs, clothe the floor in clashing rugs, hang statement curtains or paste up big graphic prints as a backdrop.

In the kitchen, it's all about the table. Soften the hard edges and industrial look of a modern kitchen with original tables and chairs from past eras. Fall in love with a cottage-style table, a Formica-top retro table, a Forties enamel top table or source an old favourite, a generously sized old wooden farmhouse table. These items are often much less expensive than their high street counterparts. If you do have a modern kitchen table, you can always give it a make-over by changing the stain, the colour or style. For example, keep the chic, sleek glass top, but add industrial trestle legs.

Tables need chairs to highlight their personalities. Make a table stand out by picking clashing chairs, mixing and matching seats of different characters, shapes, materials, and

eras. If you don't fancy single chairs, pull up an old church pew as a bench or add interest to a modern-style bench with vintage-print cushions. Bar stools are also a modern home favourite. Source old barber stools, retro diner stools or simply any that contrast with your kitchen.

Since we spend a third of our lives asleep, your bed needs the best of modern (a fresh, supportive mattress and sturdy base) and a vintage twist with bedheads or frames. Choose from a number of traditional looks – like the Napoleon or sleigh bed, popular in the mid 1800s – or look out for antique iron, 'mission' style, art deco or old wooden bed frames and give them a contemporary make-over with a funky backdrop or quirky bedding. If you've already invested in a high street buy, just give it a vintage make-over with hipster fabrics.

While the sofa, the kitchen table and the bed are your main investment buys, there are many other pieces to consider. Take storage, for example – everything needs its place! Here, again, be original and use pieces in unusual settings: an old wardrobe in a minimal modern hall for guests' coats, a set of old wooden office drawers in a bedroom for clothes storage, or an old trunk for kitchen seating with handy built-in linen storage. Bedroom drawers, painted in fresh, offbeat colours, also make excellent living room pieces. Restore order, but in an exciting old—new way.

retro chic Tim Rundle and his partner Glynn Jones, owners of this chic Seventies bungalow in Nottingham, have cherry-picked a range of eclectic furniture for this elegant living room. The armchair, chosen for its stately shape, has been upholstered in a stylish blue tweed. He's created a quiet corner where the sitter can reflect on the world outside or dip into a book aided by the light of a modern reading lamp above. Beside the chair are retro-style reproduction tables and a screen from high street store, Habitat. To make the chair look more sculptural, a piece of art in its own right, Tim has created a canvas for it in 'Mouse's Back', a neutral, but warm grey from the Farrow & Ball paint range (*left*). A tall Seventies wooden sideboard creates a handsome, eye-catching storage piece, which provides a long horizontal display area for all Tim's quirky, kitsch vintage finds (*below*).

surprise, surprise From the outside of this brick building, you'd never guess the living room would have such a light, airy feeling as sunlight streams in through huge glass walls. An enormous mirror bounces this light into every corner. It's more New York loft than the suburbs. Tim has carefully picked each piece, contrasting the moulded acrylic armchairs and a clean-lined modern table with quirky pieces, like the striking three-seater Victorian 'conversation chair'. In the corner is a modular Seventies-style sofa. An eye-catching lamp on a modern side table towers over the retro tea set beside it. The furnishings throughout are all gentle shades of pistachio, grey, pale turquoise and a soft yellow (*opposite page*).

wonderful wood Tim Rundle has taken an old set of wooden drawers (*right*) and turned them into a piece of wall art, even using them as a canvas for miniature landscapes. Throughout his modern home, oil paintings of grand, stylish men and women of yesteryear grace his walls. Old marble busts, torsos and heads are a recurring theme, seen in various rooms, bringing in a little Roman glamour and decadence. The torso on the table is guardian of the keys. Downstairs, the canvases include a glossy wooden floor and fresh white wall paint, the perfect showcase for all Tim's finds. Everything has been selected with Tim's eye for the exceptional, the glamorous and the quirky.

fabulous fifties

Textile artist Petra Boase lives in Norfolk. She has a penchant for retro and has cherry-picked pieces from a Fifties colour palette for her home, such as the pale blue cuckoo clock, the pale yellow storage cupboard and the pretty pink curtains (*far right*). Areas of pattern, like the ornamental chair, upholstered with vintage fabrics, Union Jack sink curtain (*right*) and the soft green curtains (*below*) add a splash of visual interest.

collide styles

Here, an enamel-topped utility cupboard, crowned with a three-way folding vanity mirror, collides with the woven chair in the background (*left*). To the side of the cupboard a tall handsome vintage lamp stand looks arresting and modern again with a naked bulb instead of its original shade. Pale painted floors are part of a classic, minimal Scandinavian look, making the perfect neutral canvas for furniture from any era.

recycle, reuse

This elegant high-backed sofa in the home of Anthropologie creative team, Trevor Lunn and Kristin Norris, has been reupholstered in faded vintage monogrammed linens. The couple have clashed the plain backdrop with a regal-looking cushion. Beside it, a large pile of books teeters on an old fold-out stool, making an impromptu reading corner. As the room has high ceilings, there's plenty of room for a tall, handsome, wooden display case (*opposite page*).

evoke the past

In a corridor outside French artist Claire Basler's bedroom (*left*) is a collection of mis-matched furniture, antique clocks and toys from yesteryear. Against these original, natural pieces, the chic, stylish photo by feted fashion photographer Chico Bialas stands out. In her bedroom (*above, left*), owner Sandrine Place, a French interiors stylist and consultant, has collected old chests of drawers and painted them in various shades of blues, turquoises and purples to create a unique set of storage. A trio of round paper shades provide light from above, and bring a sense of visual rhythm.

lost luggage

In the bedroom of James Russell and Hannah Plumb, the artists behind JamesPlumb, a stack of antique leather suitcases in a bespoke wooden frame provides quirky clothes storage (*right*). The sideboard in Sandrine Place's family kitchen is an old wooden cabinet, which she has re-employed and added height to with new polished chrome legs (*above right*).

stylish drawers In his signature style, Tim Rundle has re-employed an antique haberdashery cabinet as clothing storage. A wise old owl looks sagely on the room, while an elegant portrait of a grand lady in blue dress sits casually against the wall. Two intricate wooden lamp bases make a sculptural duo; in one, on a branch, two butterflies perch on either side. Wherever you look in Tim's home, you encounter his surreal sense of wit and humour (*left, top and bottom*).

open and shut Nina Tolstrup and Jack Mama, both furniture and product designers, live in London. While their home is a testament to Tolstrup's Danish roots, with a clever twist, Nina keeps their family home feeling flexible, open and flooded with daylight. One of the most surprising features is a bespoke structure made from 24 doors, creating the children's play and sleeping areas (*opposite page, right, and above*). Each of these doors has a story to tell, coming from friends, skips, anywhere and everywhere. The structure was specifically created to be easy to change by her two children. Hinges, sliders and handles mean that they can re-organize the structure to suit their play. It can be open, for an instant racetrack, or closed, making an excellent space to play hide-and-seek. The family has also sourced modern and vintage toys to suit the space. As the space is large, open and flexible, there's plenty of room to ride a bike or play chase.

lighting

Every room needs illumination, so let there be light, modern vintage style. Pick the best of the old and mix it with the new. Juxtapose swooping brushed chrome floor lamps against delicate floral shaded sidelights. Contrast old oil lamps with industrial workbench lighting. Lighting may seem a small detail, yet when all the details chime together, they create an overall symmetry that feels just right.

When sourcing light fixtures, you'll find a heady mélange of modern lights, reproduction fittings and of course originals. Get yourself up to speed on true vintage lights by spending time looking at lighting styles from different periods. When you find something you like, examine it thoroughly, looking out for old logos, manufacturer names, symbols, motifs or maker's marks. If a lamp is in good order, but needs restoration, you can always paint or restain an old base to your own taste.

Sometimes it's hard to imagine that it was only a little over 100 years ago that lighting ran on gas and oil. It wasn't until after the 1900s that electricity began to permeate into our homes. Infiltrating slowly at first, it soon became mainstream and lighting styles subsequently exploded. If you find pre-electric styles, you'll have a true, timeless antique. Being of very basic design, many oil lamps will still work (though they may need a new wick), while others are just suitable for show.

Early lighting pieces turn up in junk shops, flea markets and garage sales and, of course, on the internet. Popular examples of early electric lights include Louis Comfort Tiffany's classic stained glass shades (worth a small fortune these days), the rather elegant, but sedate lines of the Arts and Crafts period, and the more ornate designs of the art nouveau movement. With rapidly changing attitudes and tastes, the roaring Twenties saw the design of more statement pieces and the humble glass light took on different shapes, including zig zag, half-moon and sunburst shapes.

One word of warning, however, if you are choosing original pieces: make sure you buy suitable bulbs as many of these lights were not designed to take bulbs of more than 40 watts. If you like a look, but don't have the patience to update wiring or source specific bulbs, there are plenty of high street reproductions that will work with modern systems.

In the Fifties, lamps and lighting took a more modernist turn, with many of the styles still popular today, like Arco Castiglioni's elegant swan lamp and the 'space age' lamp by then directional company Rotaflex. These lights began to play with shape and proportion, like adding a large white ball to a straight tall base or an oversized mushroom shape. More recent classics, like Tom Dixon's Mirror Ball floor lamps, or the paper shades of Japanese lighting designer Isamu Noguchi, will inject modern elegance into more vintage interiors.

There's also nothing quite like the more playful lights now on the high street, like garlands of flowers or coils of glowing rope, which bring in a sense of festivity and fun.

When it comes to the overall room, your overhanging pendant light will be the most eye-catching feature. Make sure it crowns your room by covering it with your best vintage fabric or customizing it with fake flowers or beads. Large plastic globes and paper shades

bathroom beauties Lighting can transform a space from the ordinary to the extraordinary: in this bathroom (*above*), the draped cords and tiny, ornate Moroccan shades, create a bejewelled look, while the large modern polka-dotted globe brings in a soft honeyed light. On the mantelpiece (*opposite*), a stunning light with a sculptural base makes a perfect accessory.

also look striking, as do classic shapes, such as industrial or Chinese paper shades.

One style that transcends all decades is the glamorous chandelier. Often ornate, sometimes overly intricate, vintage chandeliers are valued for adding light, elegance and style, whether they're traditional Venetian drop glass chandeliers or more contemporary styles, like Tom Kirk's 'GS300'. The crystal chandelier is a favourite, once made of near-diamond quality crystals, but now looking equally beguiling with glass. Metal chandeliers are also available in a broad range of styles, from modern industrial to decorative vintage, from the worn patina of a wrought-iron chandelier to a shiny brass or contemporary chrome finish. Although reproductions are widespread, somehow nothing beats an original, which you can easily restore or customize with your own additions, like glass beads or fake flowers.

With task lighting, find the right light for the job, but give it a modern vintage twist. Ex-office lights make great reading lights, while in living rooms you'll need anglepoise lamps or well-positioned sconces. If you have a traditional pendant lamp, contrast it with a contemporary mounted wall sconce or a sleekly modern floor lamp.

Think quirky. Every era has had its lighting sense of humour. If you're after a Seventies vibe, the spaghetti swag lamp is the perfect choice. Of course, the lava lamp (or Astro lamp), invented by an Englishman, Edward Craven-Walker in the early Sixties, adds a retro feel. Back in the Thirties, soothing 'motion' lamps became all the rage, featuring popular scenes, like the 'Forest Fire with Log Cabin' and water cascading down Niagara Falls.

And customize. If you find a base you love, you can easily fashion a shade from vintage fabric to match – you just need a simple frame kit, which are easily found on the internet. Bases themselves can be given a new twist by painting them a fresh new colour. Try clashing eras or colours in your base–frame pairing.

Consider your natural lighting sources too. Maximize the daylight by making sure plenty of light filters into your home. Where light is scarce, bring in large mirrors and polished surfaces to bounce light into dark corners. Create whole walls of mirrors – mis-matching shapes and eras – to really harness the light you have. If you want to keep out prying eyes, but preserve the atmosphere, drape modern windows with vintage lace or linens.

There's nothing quite like firelight. For a vintage look, bring in early examples of hand-held or votive candle holders. Pop tealights in old, finebone china teacups or even vintage champagne bowl-shaped glasses. Old vases, crystal dessert bowls, sculpted glass bottles and coloured tumblers all make pretty, offbeat candle holders, too. Candelabras are the centrepeice of every table, so seek out antique silver examples or modern handcrafted ceramic pieces that contrast with your table. Or put a candelabra in your fireplace to transform an empty space with a beautiful soft light.

lampshades

Aurelie Mathigot creates her own finely handcrafted pieces to suit old frames she's found. She has hand-stitched crocheted flowers onto a crocheted base, leaving a soft fringe gently dangling (*top left*). Petra Boase reclaims pre-loved fabrics and creates her own floral shades, matching these dainty tops with odd bases (*top right*). Tim Rundle has taken a glamorous base, chosen a plain yet curvaceous shade and adorned it with an old brooch (*bottom left*). Almost every detail in Aurelie's home has had her gold dust sprinkled over it. Here a glass lamp wears a crocheted cover; the light will diffuse gently through the intricate pattern (*bottom right*). In the home of French interior stylist, Sandrine Place, three lamps stand together, as if deep in conversation. She has reclaimed the old bases and painted them in striking colours, then given each one a suitable hat (*opposite page*).

wallflowers On this wall, above a reading chair, a quirky fixture provides a gentle glow to read by. Three bulbs have been given a smart new lease of life and been rewired with red, silk-covered flex to fit in with the overall colour scheme. These statement pieces have been cleverly arranged to form an intriguing still life.

light fantastic

Like pieces of jewellery, use light fixtures as home accessories. Lights can masquerade as pieces of sculpture or be decorated with anything you love. In Ann Shore's home (*above left*), she has draped a collection of necklaces with strung beads and fabric flowers around a wall sconce. Three pearl-coloured shells perch above the fitting, turning this plain Jane light into something beautiful. On a wall in Derrière, a restaurant in Paris, a retro double wall light throws stripes of colour over a distressed wall, layering a pattern of light over the zigzagged wallpaper (*above right*). Above a bed, a branch of pretty flower lights trails up a wall, awaiting a Sleeping Beauty below. A wonderful wall sconce injects a feeling of romance, dreams and, of course, a soft gentle light (*right*).

leading lights

A pair of beautiful wings gives this Ingo Maurer lamp an angelic twist (*top left*). Reclaim old lights, like this industrial Jielde lamp, left in its original distressed state. By placing it on a bright yellow plinth, it becomes modern again. (*top middle*). If your lights are plain, contrast them with dramatic ceiling roses, such as this piece by JamesPlumb (*top right*). This elegant palm-fringed floor lamp was discovered in a Paris flea market (*bottom left*). Lighting can be there just to add beauty, like this amber-coloured tree set beside an ornate painting (*bottom middle*). Chandeliers, whether modern or vintage, metal or glass, inject glamour into any space in the room (*bottom right*). Avoid eyestrain with a good sidelight, like this sleek modern lamp, which is juxtaposed with the rustic, hand-sewn sofa cover and mis-matched cushions (*opposite page*).

textiles

Harness the power of textiles. In every home seen here, fabrics add warmth, colour and interest. Hand-sewn quilts, soft rugs, rough linens and delicate lace smooth out hard-edged modern homes or add a contemporary twist to more traditional abodes. On an emotional level, textiles make a home feel, well, truly like home. Thick blankets, snug curtains and piles of pillows feel cosy and comforting.

What exactly is vintage fabric? And what makes a fabric 'modern'? Retro-istas in the know refer to 'vintage' as the period between 1920 and 1980. Before 1920, fabric is considered 'antique', while after 1980, prints are deemed modern. To get the modern vintage balance, you need a broad mixture, featuring each era.

Sourcing true vintage and antique pieces involves time, patience and luck. On the internet, Google will reveal many e-stores run by passionate specialists. You'll find plenty of end-of-rolls, retro reprints and second-hand curtains, duvets, quilts and cushions on eBay or e-commerce sites like Amazon. 'Freecycle' communities, where people give away unwanted items, will often have suitable swathes and items for reuse. If you're an enthusiast, join online forums so you can meet like-minded people who will share insider knowledge about lesser-known sources.

While online sources are vast, there's nothing quite like the thrill of stumbling on a piece in an unexpected place. Look for vintage fabric at car boot sales, jumble sales, and charity shops. And, think laterally. Often an old skirt, shawl, sackcloth or army blanket can be cut into cushions or patchworked together to form a multitude of pieces. Keep your eyes out for other examples of vintage handiwork, like tea cozies, hot-water bottle covers, lace doilies or embroidered wall hangings to dot around the home.

Otherwise, revive old traditions and create your own masterpieces. Recently, knitting, sewing, macramé (so Seventies) and crochet have undergone a massive revival. Sewing cafés, knitting circles and crochet groups have sprung up everywhere. When you design your own piece, you can tailor it to your needs: try knitting a cushion cover to spruce up an old sofa, or crocheting chic table placemats.

With needle and thread, you can customize. Buy a jar of old brass buttons and sew them onto your favourite curtains or cushion for instant glamour. Old beads, pom poms, ribbons or sequins also add vintage flair to modern fabrics. Or simply take one of your gran's old brooches and glitz up a lampshade. As with clothes, fabrics look alluring when arranged in layers or contrasted together. So layer a Fifties-era chintz tablecloth over a plain modern colour on a bedside table, or create contrast with mounds of pillows, clashing texture, pattern and colour.

While vintage fabrics are the real thing, you'll also discover a multitude of fabrics at high street stores that give you the style in a textile that's often easier to look after, particularly graphic prints, 1940s cowboy prints, modern florals and Hawaiian motifs.

When it comes to prints, be bold with your mix: team paisleys with florals, stripes with graphics or polka dots, or blocks of plain colour with pattern. If you see something you love, just covet it — it will find its place.

bring back crochet In the last century, both the Fifties and the Seventies saw trends in crochet and brightly coloured yarns crafted into 'granny squares' became de rigueur. If you can't find any vintage examples, simply join a class and learn to create your own, like those on Nathalie Lete's bed (*above*). Be inspired by Aurelie Mathigot's handmade world. In her kitchen, a delicate crocheted posy looks beautiful in a crochet-covered vase (*opposite*).

When shopping, keep your eye out for unusual pieces to use in fresh ways and become an expert at deconstruction. Use tablecloths, chenille bedcovers, old dresses or sew old roll end strips together to create mis-matched curtains or bedcovers. Even vintage aprons, which featured generous pockets, can be pegged onto walls for interesting storage.

Old fur coats sewn from soft mink and rabbit were once popular. So pull your aunty's old shawl out of the dressing-up box and sew it into a soft, gorgeous cushion. Mixed with chestnut brown and white cow skins or a soft sheepskin on the floor, these old furs will feel fresh again. Faux furs and old, faded denims are also excellent modern vintage additions.

With older textiles and fabrics, be very careful about the way you clean them as some of these pieces can be very fragile or made with old dyes that may run. Lace and trims can also distort with washing. Wash delicate, vintage pieces with a gentle mild soap in lukewarm water and dry in the open air (but not in direct sunlight). Tumble-dry at your peril. Furs should be taken to professional cleaners.

Let's look at some key pieces and their uses. Quilts are so versatile and you'll find a massive variety of patterns and sizes. To add life to an armchair or sofa, throw over a colourful quilt, tucking it under the seat cushion as a casual slip cover. If your quilt is a little worn out, just patch it up or select the least worn areas to cut out and use for extra-soft cushions. Vintage quilts, particularly the old hand-sewn crib quilts, make stunning wall art. And, for an extra warm window covering, you can also sew big wooden hooks onto an old quilt, and hang it on a wooden railing as an eye-catching curtain.

Old lace, while often antique, adds a soft feminine touch wherever it is. Use it as a valance or create a beautiful window covering. Again, some hand-stitched pieces – such as babies' christening gowns, handkerchiefs, small tablecloths and vintage doilies – are so beautifully crafted, you might even consider framing them. A lace dresser scarf makes a gorgeous table runner, or adds a feminine twist to a modern sofa.

Old linens are also so versatile. Their loose weave and natural feel lends itself to a huge number of uses. Cut up old sheets into table napkins, dyeing the squares with tea for a more antique look, or use preserved strips of worn out sheets to fashion into stylish tablecloths. Old sheets also make diffuse window coverings. Vintage linen pillow covers on top of a Thirties chenille bedspread will also provide a classic contrast.

Finally, don't forget your floors. Cover wooden or stone surfaces with fabulous vintage rugs. Far Eastern or floral print rugs and flock carpets bring in a traditional look, while Verner Panton prints from the Sixties, graphic prints and stripes add a modern twist to classic floorboards or vintage patterned tiles.

And, don't forget, textiles are the one thing you can change to suit your mood or the season. Create a cosy look by leaving plenty of thick piles of rugs and cushions around for the winter, while in the summer keep your textiles to a minimum, changing cushions to something bright and breezy. Experiment.

add softness Use fabrics to add a feeling of softness, warmth and femininity to your home. A curtain in a hallway creates a pocket of pattern and colour, also acting as a room divider (*opposite page, top left*). Create your own curtains from a collage of fabrics, like the patchwork here, sewn from pieces in various patterns and colours (*top right*). Take an old lampshade frame and stretch over a fresh length of fabric (*bottom left*). Clash patterns and textures: in this bedroom, the curtains, cushions, lampshade and covers perfectly mis-match (*bottom right*).

clash your fabrics This bedspread has been handcrafted out of tiny patches of fabric, bringing in a homely, comforting feel to this bedroom. The floral cushions add to the country look, where everything feels effortlessly relaxed and casually thrown together. Achieve this feel with clusters of cushions, mixing up patterns, like polka dots and stripes, florals and paisley, graphic patterns and plain. Avoid visual overload by ensuring there is a quiet, neutral background, like the warm brown, seen here (*this page*).

homemade style

Aurelie Mathigot, an artist/designer from Paris, has literally created her own spin on modern life, right down to the details, like the hand-knitted patchwork Apple Mac cover. Instead of a cupboard door, she's created a patchwork curtain, in similar hues, to conceal an alcove of storage (*opposite page*). In the living room, Aurelie has given some long branches a quirky twist by wrapping them with fabric and rope. Her sofa, a mis-match of comfortable cushions, beckons. For a sofa cover, she's used a crocheted throw given a modern touch with brightly coloured yarns (*this page*). Throughout her home she has embroidered, sewn, knitted and crocheted everything, reclaiming the old and fashioning the new. She says her work is inspired by the notion of recovery and the necessity of creating everyday life in a new way.

original vintage

Here, a true vintage print has been transformed into an eye-catching blind above a kitchen sink. The sunlight catches the Seventies-style graphics (*top left*). A visual mis-match of feminine prints works together with a common theme of pinks, blues and soft greens (*top right*). Culture clash: a straight-laced pinstriped seat cover clashes with an elegant Japanese-print cushion (*bottom left*). Bring in textiles on items of furniture, like this funky lampshade perched on top of an old base. Unusual pairings like this become stars, standing out against plain backdrops (*bottom right*).

soft and sedate

Textiles are used in a number of ways to soften, comfort and provide visual highlights to an otherwise serene room. The lampshade, a vintage print on a reclaimed base, brings an upbeat groove into this more sedate room. A length of Seventies fabric creates a simple door curtain (*opposite page*).

go bold In this living area, a classic nut-brown cow skin adds a welcome, natural touch. The sofa has been half re-covered in a rough-weave fabric, while its more colourful companion, a sculptural armchair, has been reupholstered with bright, patterned vintage magic. Striped, yet neutral, cushions thrown on top of each piece bring a sense of visual harmony to the room.

MAD HUNGRY
cook bo

natural neutrals In the Brooklyn home of Nadia Yaron and Myriah Scruggs, natural fabrics in neutral tones – raw linens, pure cottons, rough-weave hessian and old sackcloth – add softness and light to their space (*top left*). On a sunlit day bed, a mix of extra large and small cushions in similar neutral tones plays with proportion. On the floor, a striped, graphic rug brings in colour and pattern (*below*). In the home of Dean Sawyer, vintage satin drapes at a doorway (*bottom left*).

decorating

The beauty of modern vintage decorating is in its eclectic nature. Everything is casually thrown together, yet the relaxed mis-match of finishes and colours just seems so right. Simply embrace your home's readymade quirks, like exposed brickwork, old wallpaper, peeling paint, ancient flagstones and original tiles. For this is truly your home's vintage.

When it comes to your large canvases – your walls and floors – remember that opposites attract. Contrast your decorating with your furniture to keep the balance of old and new. If you choose distressed, rag-rolled walls, a modern, white leather Barcelona day bed would be the perfect match; while if you favour a modern graphic wallpaper, juxtapose it with an antique wooden chest. By clashing the background with your pieces, you already begin the beautiful mix of modern and vintage in any location, from a chic New York loft to an old country farmhouse.

Let's start with your walls. In many homes throughout these pages, you'll see swathes of wallpaper (yes, wallpaper). In recent decades – particularly during the minimalist Nineties when strictly white walls were the fashion – papering has been a neglected art. Now, again, we're hankering for the prettiness and pattern only wallpaper can bring.

Since the days of teapot prints, fusty florals and garish graphics, wallpaper has come a long way, with many fashionable designers clamouring to put their names to fresh, original prints. While there are many modern prints, one of

the easiest ways to put vintage into your home is to seek out original rolls from past eras, often found in the usual second-hand haunts or on specialist websites. If you don't have the time or patience to source originals, many companies are doing fabulous reproductions, including some with a modern twist on old designs, such as metallic flock prints or floral patterns in minimalist black and white.

With wallpaper, walls become their own masterpieces. They're so full of pattern, any other adornments, such as mirrors or picture frames, can afford to be plain. When choosing a paper, spend time in the room. A tiny room can spark to life with a mis-match of rolls. If your room is predominantly modern, pick out a strong vintage print, like a Sixties graphic design. Or, if your look is erring towards the traditional, select something bold and contemporary. To suit your home's character, your vintage twist could always be a paper from that era; for example, if your home was built in the first two decades of the 20th century, choose an art deco-inspired print.

Of course, you don't just have to use one print throughout. Think about using patterns in vertical stripes, based around a colour theme, or creating a patchwork of prints using various paper designs. Otherwise, you may just find one wall or area can take a piece of retro pattern. In living rooms, frame fireplaces and windows with bold prints. Or, just paper one wall behind your sofa, clashing the style of the print with the seating. In kitchens, you can use it to paper cupboards or to create a splashback accent between the countertops and cupboards, however, you will need to protect this high-use area from the spills and

decorate Most of your decoration takes place on your home's big canvases, your floors and walls. Yet, it's the little details that count: patches of rough, distressed paintwork on a door, contrasted with a glass jewel of a door knob (*opposite page, right*), or a roll of wallpaper, iron table and pretty, crochet-covered lamp set against a modern, minimalistic white room (*above*). It is this disparity that makes modern vintage truly work.

splashes with a matte sealer. As in living rooms, a papered accent wall behind the bed creates an alluring backdrop, while in bathrooms, the wall behind a plain sculptural tub can come to life with a soft floral or bold graphic pattern.

Wallpaper doesn't just have to live on walls. You can use it to decorate all sorts of other areas, large or small. Room dividers or screens also enliven plain spaces when clothed with striking prints. Use a montage of papers to cover old wardrobes, vanity units or stacks of storage boxes. Plain pails, vases, book covers and other details can also benefit from a splash of vintage wallpaper. Of course, decorative wallpapers can function as wall art all on their own. Simply choose an elegant pattern and mount it in a contrasting frame.

If wallpapering seems too much, paint will do the trick. As modern vintage is relaxed and a little careworn, your paintwork can be relaxed too. Distressed wall paint easily creates the feel of a lived-in space. Simply prepare your walls, painting them with a base colour (this doesn't have to be flawless). When the paintwork has dried, create a textured, old-worldly feel by removing areas of the base coat by sanding. For an authentic touch, you'll need to create random spots that are a variety of sizes to make the original surface visible. If you like the look of more ancient finishes, mix plaster, apply it in swirls and scrape some of it away to create the 'worn away' feeling. If you like painting, or know someone who does, you can also paint murals directly onto walls.

When decorating, choosing the right colour is essential. Paint a 'test patch' (about a metre square) and live with it for a few days. This is particularly important with strong colours, which can elicit a powerful emotional punch. Pick and mix colours from the eras. The Fifties were all about soft pastels (such as baby pink, apple green, sky blue); the Sixties went psychedelic (hot pink, deep turquoise, dark purple); and the Seventies became all warm and natural (think olive green, burnt orange and fresh mustard). Otherwise, choose timeless, classic colour pairings, like white and blue. For a mid-century, yet still modern look, go monochrome with sophisticated black and white.

In older homes, hidden underneath contemporary floor coverings, lie many vintage treasures. If you are unsure what your carpet or linoleum is laid over, peel up a corner and check for classic wooden floorboards or beautiful vintage tiles that can be restored. Today, many ceramic tiles are the most unremarkable squares, used to create tidy, easy-to-clean surfaces. However, a century ago, tiles were hand-painted with vibrant colours, intricate patterns and all sorts of motifs to create hard-wearing but decorative floors. These were the art of the everyday and, thanks to vintage, tile style is back. Original vintage and reproduction tiles are in demand again and are being used in new spaces within the home, like kitchen splashbacks, bathroom surrounds, on cupboards and simply as wall art. You can source these from specialist shops, but you'll also discover old examples in salvage yards. Revive the old and beautiful.

natural tones The rough and ready paintwork in this home adds to its natural, earthy feel. Here, Nadia Yaron and Myriah Scruggs have painted a dark colour up to the dado line, where they have rolled on a khaki colour in a loose, carefree manner. Then, by taking a light colour to the ceiling, the whole room feels lifted, light and airy. They have kept the original wood floorwork with its beautiful geometric patterns (*opposite page*).

rough and smooth In the amazing home of French artist Claire Basler, rough and smooth, masculine and feminine, contemporary and antique, clash side by side. To keep a sense of history, she has left some walls in their distressed state, leaving peeling patches of original paintwork (*above*). As you walk through her doorways, you come to her living room, where the walls are painted in coal black, the perfect masculine backdrop for her flowery, pretty paintings. Her floorboards are left raw, natural and unpolished (*right*).

beautiful blooms In every room in Claire Basler's home are beautiful bunches of floral decoration. Whether real or painted onto large canvases, she surrounds herself with wild flowers, bringing the countryside into her home. To highlight her paintings, she's created a petrol blue backdrop, so everything light, like the vintage linen pillows, looks fresh and bright.

bright sparks In the Sixties, maverick designer Verner Panton brought a psychedelic colour palette into homes. In the Philadelphia home of Trevor Lunn and Kristin Norris, bright walls hark back to Panton's palette, contrasting an acid green with a shiny red plastic chair and a black and white graphic rug. The contrasting patterns on the bed soften the overall feel, and the neutral white plastic table and white sheets add just the right amount of plain (*left*). Striking red and pink walls bring a sense of high drama to David Alhadeff's bedroom. The patchwork quilt and a plain side table create quiet, homely contrasts (*above*).

roll up, roll up

Doyenne of textiles, Petra Boase has collected old rolls of vintage wallpaper and created an eye popping wall of mis-matched patterns. While the overall feel is eclectic, all the rolls have a common rhythm and theme of graphic florals in yellows, oranges, blues and greens, which creates an overall harmony (*right*). If you don't feel daring enough to paper a whole room, try just papering one wall of accent colour and pattern. Tim Rundle has papered a sliding wall divider with pretty blue florals, bringing a soft, glamorous touch into his bedroom (*below*).

layer upon layer

David Alhadeff is the owner of Future Perfect, a shop that reflects his passion for design innovation and craftsmanship. In his dining room, the canvas is a striking wall of mis-matched vintage wallpapers, while the floor is painted in a neutral tone. Using a montage of textures, David injects a little romance into this former warehouse, where he has lived for almost a decade. His table juxtaposes sleek glass with industrial trestle legs, while a mish-mash of chairs in different styles clashes a myriad of textures. Here Philippe Starck's transparent 'Louis Ghost' chair rubs shoulders with a retro leather armchair and a pair of strictly utilitarian dining chairs. Crowning the table is a duo of antique vases, softened by tall, fresh hydrangeas. Above hangs a curvaceous, modernist pendant lamp. In order to retain the loft's industrial feel, David has sourced matching chrome appliances, including a toaster and a blender (*right*).

pretty pattern

All of these pictures show how areas of vintage pattern bring a sense of the past into modern homes. Once, the humble tile was the everyday art in a home, seen on floors and walls (*above, top left and right*). In her kitchen (*opposite*), French textile artist Aurelie Mathigot has taken old white and blue tiles and used them to decorate splashbacks, contrasting these pretty tiles with modern brushed aluminium. Pretty door handles also add contrast. An interesting idea is to bring in pattern with a roll of wallpaper, but to use it as a wall-hanging, leaving the roll unfurled (*above, top middle*). Montages, patchworks and unusual prints, made from wrapping paper, vintage posters and old magazines also create areas of pattern. Just choose a colour or pattern theme and find as many examples as you can to clash together (*above, bottom row*).

collections
& display

In each and every one of us,
there's a passionate collector
waiting to be set free, whether
we're aware of it or not. As
you'll see from these pages, all
these homeowners have let their
hoarder run riot. Their passion
for kitsch creatures, zany toys,
pretty blooms and hip art has
been let out to create inspired
collections that are artfully
displayed. Modern
vintage gives you
permission to unlock
your passion and find it
in as many shapes and forms
as you can.

French artist Claire Basler feels she must always live with the outdoors inside, decorating her home with painted or fresh flowers, while English textile designer Petra Boase collects vintage wallpapers, foraging for precious prints everywhere and anywhere. English homeowner Tim Rundle collects odd creatures, like tiny squirrels, plastic deer and porcelain horses; French artist/designer Nathalie Lete is wild about reviving old toys or creating them herself out of vintage fabrics.

To create your own collection, decide what you feel truly, madly, passionately about, then challenge yourself to find the quirkiest, most classic, or just the most outstanding piece in its genre. Your passion could be perfume bottles, souvenirs collected from cities you've loved, colourful biscuit tins, hand mirrors, unusual vases, or even bigger items, like strictly Sixties furniture, or vintage leather chairs in various shapes. Every piece has a story to tell. To get inspiration, look at what you already have. If you've got more than three pieces, your collection is underway.

Then the fun begins, as you track down these things in a Miss Marple-like manner. When your friends discover your collection, they will join in, acting as scouts, sourcing and reporting coveted finds. You'll sometimes pick up pieces in the most unexpected places, often when you're not even looking. Many you will unearth at flea markets, jumble sales, car boot sales, second-hand shops or even on street corners. A number of high street and boutique shops have some rather surprising finds too, as retro pieces become hip again and designers rediscover old crafts and fashion pieces in new and exciting ways. If you would rather shop from home, there's always the internet – eBay is the obvious choice for a constant source of surprises.

Once you have gathered your assortment, think about clever ways to display the items – an art in itself. Find something that unites the pieces and cluster them together, allowing enough space to give them room to breathe. It might be a colour scheme that brings them together, or a particular era or theme, such as Seventies coffee pots or stacks of pretty floral fabrics. This way, collections of objects become almost like families, all individual, but definitely from the same set of genes.

Multiples of things often create a soothing sense of rhythm, even in the pedestrian and everyday, like a row of milk bottles or stools, or a line-up of antique teapots. If you've fallen for Sixties coffee pots, put them in a row, take off the lid and pop in big bright blooms to give them a fresh new look.

Walls are the perfect canvas for all sorts of collections. Create show-stopping wall displays by hanging *objets d'art*: everything from old keys, clocks, necklaces, vintage dresses, scarves and even Christmas baubles create impromptu areas of visual interest.

the big clash Make sure your coveted collections are displayed where they can bask in all their glory, ensuring the backdrops around are plain or neutral. Whenever you can, collide eras and styles: a strictly modern graphic painting sits in an ornate, gilt-edged frame (*above*). Ria Charisse clusters together old and modern *objets d'art*, like the once popular, pinned dragonflies, an heirloom photograph and a brass rabbit (*opposite page*).

Art can be displayed in tune with modern vintage style. Choose pieces along a theme, then collect examples of these from every era, like Victorian horses and modern horse prints or old-fashioned floral oil paintings and modern floral prints. Hang prints or paintings in visually exciting ways, such as pinning them along a string with old wooden pegs or chunky bulldog clips. Otherwise, choose mis-matched frames to clash with the pictures, putting a modern print in a gilt-edged frame or a vintage picture in a clean-lined white frame. The contrast will give a traditional print a new lease of life. You could even leave framed works freestanding, lined up along a hallway.

We all need mirrors to gaze in, but also to bring in a sense of light and space. Turn your mirrors into a collection by putting different styles of frames together on a wall, clashing past eras with contemporary design.

Many vintage lovers also dress with the same flair, so display clothes and accessories instead of hiding them behind wardrobe doors. Create shelves for statement shoes, hang your bags from Victorian hooks or place your hat collection on a vintage hat stand. Display your best vintage dress by hanging it outside your wardrobe or drape your scarf collection from hooks dotted along a wall.

Most of us have a collection of books, so put them to good use. Create stacks of books and pop an old tray on top to create an impromptu table, or pile them high in unexpected corners. Some of the photographs from your large glossy print books might be better papering a wall. In times gone by, books were almost like artworks, titles etched in gold on rich leather: leave these on a coffee table where they can be admired. Or

contrast stacks of vintage comics beside a modern living room sofa.

Many of these collections can live on any horizontal space, including mantelpieces, corner shelves, or side tables. But they can also live, vintage style, in less conventional homes: stacked wine boxes, old gym lockers and mail-sorting shelves make open pigeon holes for all your precious finds. If you put them in unexpected places, like on kitchen walls, on top of bathroom cabinets, or hallway tables, they'll have an element of visual surprise. Display your passions in prominent places where you can enjoy them: look at them every day and remember what makes you happy.

on show London creative Ann Shore knows that every collection needs its own special place: heirloom pieces and junk shop finds cluster on bespoke shelving, while old paintings and ornate wooden panels are perched on the floor (*this page*). Display your beautiful items that might otherwise have been tucked away, like this vintage collection of pearls (*opposite, top left*). Ann has a penchant for soft, pretty pictures of roses, which she leaves unframed on a wall above her desk (*opposite, bottom right*). She has also sourced more beautiful finds, like books, flower garlands, jewellery and a piece of gorgeous glassware to create a soft feminine corner.

find and collect

A collection of tin drums, odd short chairs and stools, unusual cushions and colourful bunting add a vibrant eclectic feel to this wall in the studio of French artist Nathalie Lete. Nathalie loves rescuing children's pieces and making them feel at home again (*above*).

unlikely marriage Kristin Norris and Trevor Lunn collect pieces that are striking, original and elegant, then pair them with their opposite. On this dining table, a masculine sculptural vase and an elegant wine decanter make an unusual marriage work. Look for pieces that are already examples of a collection, like this striking sculpture of old disused clocks, seen in the hall of their home (*opposite page, below left and right*).

past lives Evoke a sense of nostalgia by collecting redundant drawers and filling them with old fabrics, pin cushions, thimbles or find old files and notebooks. Stack them in higgledy piggledy piles, like these leaning towers, seen in the London home of James Russell and Hannah Plumb (*below*).

cheap chic The home of Nadia Yaron and Myriah Scruggs was created on a shoe-string. Their Brooklyn dwelling has become an experimental space for their designs; the duo work with salvaged wood, fabric scraps and other pieces. Ever inventive, here small piles of vintage books become horizontal surfaces for other pieces, like the old striped jug. Above, hangs a painting from their collection: a portrait of Nadia, painted by Myriah, which truly personalizes their original home (*above*).

think differently

Make your collection look original by displaying it in a lateral way. A heavy old drawer perched on a tower of books becomes an attractive table, while two hooks create a home for Nathalie Lete's collection of necklaces (*left*).

ways to display

A collection of wicker hats adorn a wall; a small brooch of Christmas holly becomes an unusual lampshade accessory; a collection of brass decorations create striking wall art; a hallway becomes a gallery of *objets trouvés* at the home of jewellery designer Ria Charisse; a montage of antique bottles, kitsch souvenirs and metallic flowers create an impromptu still life; in Derrière, a Parisian restaurant, a collection of old mirrors in distressed gilt-edged frames create a feeling of faded glamour (*opposite page, clockwise from top left*).

create clusters Pick a theme and look for similar pieces, creating your own special collections. On a plain wall, a quartet of butterfly pictures adds a sense of glamour to Ria Charisse's eclectic bathroom, complete with chandelier, white pebble splashback and vintage linen towels (*above left*). James Russell and Hannah Plumb decorate a window with an old printing screen (*above, top right*). In French artist Claire Basler's house, huge flowers are strewn everywhere, whether they're living, dried or painted. Dried hydrangeas and a huge floral canvas create drama on a wall (*above, bottom right*). As in nature, Claire creates a sense of rhythm by lining up collections of old bottles and filling them with purple and white irises. With a large painting of a woodland in the background, the interior almost feels like a living, breathing meadow (*opposite page*).

bookworm Almost everyone has a collection of books: instead of displaying them on a traditional shelf, do something original. In Nina Tolstrup's bedroom (*above*), books are interspersed with oddments and other collections, like vases and vintage toys. Bookshelves are drunkenly pitched at all angles on the wall in Parisian restaurant Derrière (*right*). On the bookshelf in the home of artist Claire Basler (*opposite page*), large coffee-table books are colour coded, so the whole piece becomes a floor-to-ceiling work of art.

childhood

With modern vintage, your past becomes part of your décor. After all, your home is a record of all the things you've loved. Nathalie Lete's cabinet evokes a personal history with old clocks, piggybanks, formerly loved dolls, dinosaurs and once adored stuffed toys.

memories If you find old toys in a market, but they're missing an eye, an arm or they're stark naked, follow Nathalie Lete's example and make them new again with a fresh piece of clothing and a couple of buttons (*above left*). Aurelie Mathigot uses this cabinet to display once loved toys and quirky pieces of memorabilia (*above right*). Create little areas of surprise and unexpected nostalgia on bookshelves or tiny nooks, like Petra Boase's collection of kitsch, cute woodland deer (*right*).

style

cook & eat

The modern vintage cook–eat space is the beating heart of the home. It juxtaposes the best of modernity with chic classics. Unlike the kitchens of yesteryear, we have many convenient, time-saving, hi-tech devices, yet it still makes sense to bring in a twist of vintage to inject wit, history and nostalgia. For every home needs a sense of humour and a little soul.

The best kitchens incorporate brilliant details, perfect finishes and utilitarian functionality. Kitchens are practical, hardworking spaces which can be given style and personality when the correct balance of modern and vintage is struck. Although the details are important, start by searching for materials with clean, sleek lines to prevent the space from looking over-cluttered, and build up from there.

One of the easiest ways to bring modern vintage into your kitchen is with your cabinetry.

You can either source old cabinets from local salvage or junkyards, or give existing cabinets a twist by decorating the doors with pretty, antique tiles, matte-sealed vintage wallpapers or industrial-style surfaces. A quick, low-cost fix is to simply secure old glass knobs, colourful china handles or pewter cabinet pulls to modern cupboards.

Otherwise, remove your cupboard doors entirely and keep vintage-style crockery, glassware, tea sets and other period pieces on display. Glass-fronted cupboard doors also showcase your finds. In traditional French country kitchens, the area below the kitchen sink was often disguised with a gathered curtain. For this look, source vintage fabrics in pretty florals or checks. Or go completely modern with bold graphics or giant polka dots.

Worktops are the honed muscle of the kitchen. Hardworking wood – seen in old butcher's blocks – has been a favourite for centuries, bringing in warm, honeyed hues to any kitchen. Stainless steel, however, has a slick, contemporary utilitarian feel, perfect for contrasting vintage details. If you're replacing your worktops, consider laminates. These surfaces have come such a long way from their Fifties heyday, coming now in a huge range of colourways, and instantly add retro flair.

With so many hours being spent in the kitchen, floors need to be hard-wearing and easy to clean as well as attractive. Linoleum has recently made a comeback as it's natural, easy to install and comes in a huge range of designs. Unused rolls of vintage linoleum from the Twenties to the Fifties can often be found at salvage companies or in specialist stores, but there are now modern versions that come in vintage prints. Cork was extremely popular in the Twenties and gives a wonderful warmth underfoot. Of course wooden flooring, in any condition, is a firm favourite, straddling both vintage and modern styles.

Tiles are great for adding a little twist of modern or vintage to walls. Zing up a plain wall with a pocket of busily patterned tiles or create a solid colour block of tiles in a retro colour, such as apple green or mustard. Glazed tiles reflect light, adding vivacity to your kitchen. Use them in unexpected places, such as on cupboard doors and worktops.

think different Covet pieces of furniture that are not necessarily 'kitchen furniture', like Dean Sawyer's open, industrial-style unit (*above*). Kristin Norris groups an original medicine cabinet, an old clock and a trio of ex-factory stools, which make excellent breakfast bar perches (*opposite*). To evoke a sense of yesteryear, seek out examples of vintage cookware, antique linen tea towels, old storage bottles and other classic pieces.

Bring in colour by displaying vintage cookware, serve ware and tools (think coffee grinders, retro blenders, old flour sifters, etc.) in your favourite period colours. Like the Sixties? Then go graphic black and white with your tiles and accessorize with harvest gold, burnt orange and olive green vases and teapots. If you prefer a Fifties look, think pastels: soft pink Smeg fridge, candy green tile splashbacks and baby blue crockery.

Keep your eye out too for vintage cookware, like large enamel teapots, big copper pans and those details, like old nutcrackers, French herb cutters and marble chopping boards.

Once the food is prepared, the kitchen is abandoned and it's time to eat. A dining room can be a place for formal dinner parties, as they were in the past, but most of us use it for our everyday life: a place for breakfast, homework, work, afternoon tea with friends as well as a family meal. Their purpose changes throughout the day like a tide, ebbing and flowing with people and activities.

A large, generous table is always welcoming, yet so many modern tables feel lifeless. Vintage instantly injects soul. Transform a chic tabletop with industrial-style or trestle legs. Or equally, replace a dull wooden tabletop with a colourful glass or enamel top. For a temporary change, throw over a vintage tablecloth. With small rooms, choose tables with glass or coloured laminate tops that reflect the light, making rooms seem more spacious. Old wooden tables, repainted doors or even a series of reclaimed timber planks can create a retro feel.

Mis-matched chairs, stools and benches look funky pitched side by side. Leather Sixties chairs, Parisian café chairs, industrial metal

chairs or just pretty painted chairs look like old friends when seated together. You can create a sense of unity by painting them all in one colour. Fabric seats can be reupholstered with vintage fabrics or try creating tie-back cushions from hipster prints.

The crowning piece of any table is the light above it. This is your perfect chance to inject modern vintage: suspend a glamorous chandelier over a utilitarian table or hang a clean-lined, modern pendant shade over a worn, rustic table.

When the table isn't in use, make sure you accessorize it with retro vases, antique candelabras or elegant fruit bowls to create an air of opulence. Tabletops make the perfect showcase for all your remarkable finds.

If you have space, sideboards by the dining table are useful for your serve ware. Wooden Sixties sideboards, old office cabinets or simply modern pieces create an eye-catching surface for display. Again, you can add an interesting handle or cover the front in vintage wallpaper. Accent vintage or modern barware on top, like antique cocktail shakers, soda bottles and bowl-shaped champagne glasses, presented on an antique silver tray.

Serve your food modern vintage style with antique silver cutlery, old photographic placemats, reclaimed linen napkins and vintage tumblers. Put your water in old milk bottles or ceramic milk jugs and eat, drink and be very, very merry!

utilitarian chic

In the kitchen of French textile artist Aurelie Mathigot, the colour palette is strictly white, blue and metallic. She has used pretty vintage tiles around her cupboards, so the bottom half of the room feels light and airy. On top of her cupboards, against a darker backdrop, a collection of vintage teapots are lined up, drawing the eye upwards and making the ceiling seem higher. One of her dainty, hand-crocheted vases adds a little prettiness to the utilitarian benches (*left*).

inventive style

This eating area is in the home of Kristin Norris and her husband, Trevor Lunn, creative directors at hipster store Anthropologie. Their Philadelphia home mixes the handcrafted and the machine made, glass and chrome, art and industrial. Contrasted against the utilitarian-style table and chairs is a glamorous handmade chandelier, crafted from wood and glass beads. In the background, an old silk-screen cloth has been reincarnated as wall art (*opposite page*).

airy and light Tim Rundle's dining area has a sedate feel, with plenty of white space surrounding it. The dining table, pendant lights and layered coffee table are from contemporary interiors stockist, Atomic. To complement the Sixties wooden sideboard, Tim has sourced German pressed-wood chairs from eBay. He marries the high street pieces with junkshop finds and finishes the look with chic, contemporary pieces (*below*).

modern retro The brushed granite worktop in this kitchen makes a reflective surface for Nottingham homeowner Tim Rundle's fabulous finds. He's created a still life in yellow, black and white with an array of fake mimosa flowers in a vintage glass bottle, a plastic doily and two 1950s Swedish ceramic pieces: a vegetable dish and a marmalade pot. The wall of black tiles, from Italian tile company Porcelanosa, creates a stunning backdrop. These tiles are made to look like slate and are grouted with a black finish (*left*). In contrast, the sleek white units are bought from IKEA. To make the area feel like it's floating, Tim created a cantilevered effect, taking the African hardwood flooring up underneath the cabinets. To give the dining room a twist of grandeur, he's sourced a Louis XIV sun-style mirror, which adds a little decadence (*above*). His home isn't something that's been bought 'off the shelf'. Rather, it's the story of years of collecting and sourcing things he loves.

blue and white London based creative Ann Shore has put together a striking kitchen with her fresh, arresting palette of white and blue. She has used small pieces of masking tape to cover the fridge in a montage of blue and white images, including old magazine spreads, postcards and printed photos from around the world (*above*). Carrying on this theme, Ann has papered her breakfast bar stools – made from tall cardboard storage boxes – in recommissioned pages from books and magazines, to create a patchwork of memory and nostaglia. Her granite worktop on the cooking island carries on the theme, juxtaposed with crisp white cupboards. Wooden bowls and chopping boards bring in a sense of nature, like pieces of driftwood on a seashore, and contrast with the modern, polished-aluminium extractor hood (*right*).

chair clash In these dining areas (*left and below*), both homeowners have used an odd assortment of chairs. Wooden chairs, leather armchairs, contemporary plastic chairs, IKEA finds and even an old crate make interesting dining companions. Big tables like this become more than just dining areas, but spaces where activities ebb and flow throughout the day: in the kitchen below, a tower of sticky tape, scissors and big pot of stationery are as at home as the fruit bowl. Following the eclectic theme, mix up your accessories, like coffee pots, toasters and kettles, with classic examples from other eras.

smart spaces In the Parisian home of artist Cécile Daladier and architect/designer Nicolas Soulier (*above*), the kitchen sink is integrated into the dining table, doubling up as a cook's work surface when not an eating area. Quirky finds, like a silver Aladdin's teapot on top of the cabinets and the handmade bowls (*detailed left*), create areas of visual interest. Overall, they've kept the colour scheme white, giving this bijou space a sense of airiness.

American French

In the Brooklyn home of art director and interior designer Dean Sawyer and his partner Steve Drum, quirky vintage pieces sit alongside the modern. There's a hint of French Provence in this eating area for two, with the French café-style chairs and the colour scheme of a Van Gogh painting: all warm yellows, oranges and greens (*left*). Reuse interesting pieces wherever you find them, like the old tea trolley (*below right*), which acts as a serving table. Rescue mis-matched antique cutlery from vintage markets and give pieces their job back. Nothing beats real silver cutlery (*below left*).

urban country

In Dean and Steve's kitchen, there's a distinct country feel, seen in the old enamel teapots, the thick frying pans and the striped floral sink curtain. The brickwork and piping have been painted in a fresh clean white, providing a plain backdrop for eclectic textiles (*opposite page*).

pretty in pink Kitchens can be the perfect place to show off your flair for finds, like Petra's mug collection, which includes the Queen's Silver Jubilee commemorative mugs as well as some graphic contemporary examples. Against a tiled backdrop, four quirky characters stand to attention. She's given her pieces their very own pink shelf so they have a special showcase in her home (*left*).

retro to go In the family home of Petra Boase, a top British stationery and gift designer, she has created a cook–eat area that's full of modern vintage chic. Petra employed a carpenter friend to fashion a bespoke kitchen with a Fifties vibe, including colours from the era like the candy pink shelf, the baby blue flour tin and sugar jar, and the apple green splashback. A generously sized butler's sink, with a Union Jack curtain, and a Sixties patterned fabric blind add to the eclectic-yet-hip style. While there is plenty of overall lighting from modern spotlights dotted around the ceiling, Petra has created her own funky lamp by reupholstering lampshades with retro prints and pairing them with unusual bases. With a family of three children, the table becomes a place for study and catching up on work and the day's events (*opposite page*). The doorway (*right*) is curtained with an original fabric from the Seventies.

country kitchen In the home of artist Claire Basler (*previous page, left*), flowers are in abundance. Above the old vintage butler's sink, blooms line up in re-employed grocery bottles. In brown enamel containers, she's stacked her vintage silverware, found at market places, while a lemon yellow teapot resides on the hob. Claire shows off twists of must-have modernity, like the coffee machine and an industrial-style light to assist with food preparation. Her dining table (*previous page, right*) is exactly what you'd expect: huge and country-style with elegant legs, wicker chairs and blooms of flowers to welcome guests. All the serving plates, crockery and dishware are on display, as each piece has been carefully collected for its style, vintage looks and purpose.

top tables Invest in the right table. Or make your own. Old wooden beams have been crafted together to make a rustic-style table in Parisian restaurant Derrière, accessorized with contrasting chairs, like these rather elegant, fabric-covered dining chairs with glamorous brass studs (*opposite page*). A bright pink glossy table top with polished chrome legs brings modern glamour into this dining area. It juxtaposes with the exposed brickwork, the wooden floors and the low-hanging utilitarian light (*above*). In the home of James Russell and Hannah Plumb, the table is a country-style wood, again with mis-matching wooden chairs. A single bloom arranged in a rustic bottle makes an excellent dining companion (*left*).

live

Modern vintage living combines contemporary comfort with classic chic. This is where we are truly ourselves, a space where we entertain, talk, read, or just slip into the soft hug of an armchair at the end of a long working day. This space can be public, a welcoming space for guests, or private, a quiet retreat just to think and daydream. And this is where the modern vintage look works so well, creating a lived-in style with the right mix of old charm and modern luxury.

Living spaces start with the humble hallway, an area that's often overlooked. Not here. For the majority of homes, the hallway is the first thing that greets you. But while in most homes you'll simply walk through it, in the homes featured here, the hall is the start of a journey into modern vintage style. It's time to reclaim this forgotten space and make it a place to be remembered. First impressions count.

Firstly, make it functional, yet in a beautiful way: enable your guests to easily hang hats, umbrellas and coats on vintage coat stands, old hooks or in huge antique wardrobes. Most hallways need a side table for mail, keys and other day-to-day detritus, so choose a strictly modern plastic table or an antique piece and put contrasting accessories on top: brushed aluminium containers or vintage biscuit tins for keys; antique trays with silver paperknives; old visitor's books and other *objets trouvés*. It's also the perfect place to crown a huge Sixties vase or a chic, contemporary piece of glassware and fill it with welcoming fresh flowers.

With any hallway, use elements of surprise along the walls, like a collection of jewellery, a montage of family portraits or an assortment of mis-matched mirrors. Drape garlands of lights or fake flowers, or simply choose sculptures or quirky finds, like elegant chairs, an ornate wrought-iron bookcase or old paintings propped up along the corridor. Repetitions of things, like old bottles, tins, hand-held

mirrors or anything you love, look fabulous adorning floors or walls. Clothe the floors with colourful hall runners or pull back new carpets to reveal old tiled floors to bring back your home's vintage glamour.

Every hallway opens out onto a living room. This is the one public space in the house where friends, family and visitors meet. But as with all things vintage, furnishing your living room doesn't have to be expensive. Think second-hand and collect pieces from salvage yards, junk shops, car boot sales and the internet, or simply customize your existing pieces.

Before you start, spend time throughout the day in your living room and decide on a colour scheme, thinking about the period you'd like to reference or the feel you'd like to create. Use paint or wallpaper to play with the proportions of the room: taking one colour up to the dado line and another to the ceiling will make small rooms look larger.

Whatever size your room, vintage is often about how you treat your large canvases: your floors and walls. You could source rolls of retro wallpaper to bring in colour, perhaps just covering one wall so that the pattern doesn't dominate. If your paintwork is slightly distressed, cracked or peeling, keep it that way and use modern furniture to contrast its wise, old looks. Many rooms can take a darker colour and this is where vintage's more colourful periods, the Sixties and Seventies, can come to life. For example, imagine a Seventies orange leather sofa contrasted against a charcoal wall, or a white leather Barcelona chair contrasted against a Fifties pastel green backdrop.

One of your most important purchases will be the sofa, so pick carefully from the period

spaces to think Living spaces are public and private. Create spaces in quiet, out-of-the-way retreats, like the desk and chair, opposite. Find corners, like landings, alcoves or simply section off a corner of the living room and make a place just to daydream. For all the great things you do start as a daydream so make sure you create a nook just to let your mind wander…

you like. You'll find plenty of old sofas in second-hand shops, including Sixties coloured leather sofas, country-style floral sofas and Seventies low slung black leather sofas. If you like the shape but aren't sure about the finish, you can always have these reupholstered or just cover them with a throw. It's easy to accessorize a vintage or modern sofa: dress them up with piles of mis-matched cushions flung together, including stripes, florals, graphic prints and block colours in retro shades. Cover worn out patches and snuggle up with pure wool tartan knits or army surplus blankets, or even big scarves.

There are plenty of alternatives to sofas, including the classic chaise longue, day beds and wide, wide armchairs. Again, you can always buy second-hand and reupholster them with retro prints. Singular chairs, including stools, beanbags and Moroccan-style pouffes can mean a more flexible seating space as you can move them around, creating intimate circles or seats for more guests.

Every living room needs good storage. Before TVs entered our lives, rooms were full of books. So accommodate them in wall-to-ceiling bookshelves, pile them high in disused fireplaces or just stack them along walls. To add a little vintage vibe to pre-made bookshelves, pop your things in old wicker baskets or tins, or if you've got traditional built-in bookcases, add sleek, chic vases or leather storage boxes.

Once-upon-a-time, everything was transported by ships, packed in old tea chests and trunks. In modern living rooms, these grand dames make a great flat surface to use as an impromptu coffee or side table that doubles up as storage for blankets or toys. Old leather

suitcases, in various sizes and colours, all stacked together, also add a touch of yesteryear.

Displaying your treasures where you can relax and enjoy them is most important. So make sure you create areas of visual interest, whether it's your vintage vase collection, old souvenirs, family portraits or your candelabras.

Lighting in a living room is everything. By day, you'll want to maximize the light as much as possible, so ensure you have window coverings you can pull right back, without letting in prying eyes. Curtains are a bright way to bring in a vintage colour, sourced from reproduction or original fabric rolls. Otherwise, classics like Venetian blinds nod to both the old and the new.

By night, a single pendant will provide an overall light, as will a quirky chandelier – with a little old world glamour thrown in. But readers will also want their own lamps and there's nothing quite like a large retro fabric lampshade for a bit of funk. With accent lighting, opt for colourful industrial floor lamps or modern glass lamps for a traditional interior, while for modern interiors think about choosing mis-matched shades and bases.

And then relax and enjoy yourself as life flows seamlessly around you in your modern vintage space.

make an entrance

Jewellery designer and artist Ria Charisse lives in Brooklyn. Her entrance way is no ordinary 'hello'. She's created a feeling of space by cutting out windows of light above the doorway and in the middle of the door (*opposite page*). A grand wall is adorned with a montage of intriguing finds that share a common theme: fabulous frames. She's collected hand-mirrors, natural objects, small mirrors and animal prints (*above left*). Her hat collection hovers by the doorway on hooks (*above centre*), while a stone-topped side table is home to honey-coloured glassware (*above right*). As you walk down this hallway in Parisian restaurant Derrière, the windows are covered with pieces of delicate lace to let in the light. The wooden floors are exposed, yet areas of pattern grab your attention with chequered tiles. A textured silver wall lends a glamorous air (*right*).

sculptural showcase

In the entrance to Kristin Norris and Trevor Lunn's home (*above*), a large 'clock' sculpture makes a striking appearance. Hallways are often the perfect place for unusual objects or ornate pieces of show furniture. Even though this space is open plan, they've used different floor coverings to delineate the two areas. Warm, rustic tiles make a practical covering for this hallway. Along a wall (*right*), Kristin has displayed her collection of funky necklaces, all from different eras, countries and styles. She has created her own wall art with strings of beads, chains and pendants, providing a sense of life and ornament to an otherwise plain Jane space. A funky retro side table contrasts with vintage tin and chic containers on top.

brighter bunting

A little strip of colourful bunting injects colour into a minimalist space in the French home of Cécile Daladier and Nicolas Soulier. To maximize the light, a long window provides plenty of daylight, which reflects off smooth white surfaces into this architectural space.

natural canvas In French artist Claire Basler's living room, huge canvases of flowers dominate (naturally). On the rustic, wooden floor, a rope light brings in a twist of the contemporary, along with the chic, black leather sofa and articulated floor lamp (*previous page, left*). An area has been tailor-made for relaxing, with a soft velvet day bed adorned with floral cushions, while strips of red linen bring in an injection of warmth and colour (*previous page, right*).

sitting pretty This dainty sofa is perfectly at home in the living room of Sandrine Place, an interior stylist from Paris. It's a timeless classic, yet looks fresh and modern amongst the things around it, including a funky cushion and the palm-frond lamp. Every home needs a sense of humour, which is why the rabbit lamp raises an eyebrow, making visitors feel at ease while seated on the formal chair. The background is a perfect neutral to highlight the sofa's rhythmic shape (*above*).

fabulous florals Ann Shore makes her living room oh-so pretty with plenty of textiles. She's strewn lace cushions, lace tablecloths, floral throws and vintage bedcovers over her sofa to create a soft, feminine feel. She's continued the theme with pretty paintings, postcards, fake rose stems and an old enamel jug. Even the grand mirror's frame has delicate flowers around its edges. She's also dressed up one of her mirrors, adorning it with necklaces, garlands and flowers.

culture clash In the home of Petra Boase, textiles clash and combine. She mixes everything from polka dots to stripes and florals to graphics. This texture and colour is set against neutral canvases: a wooden floor and a plain, soft grey wall. She's thrown a black sheepskin on the sofa and given it a new lease of life with funky cushions, while the armchairs have been reupholstered with patterned fabrics. The mix of lighting, a yellow industrial floor lamp, the tall elegant polka dot crowned floor lamp and the central pendant light, accessorize perfectly. The Sixties-style coffee table, the side table and the armchairs are all from the same era, which is why they work so well together (*left*). Petra has placed a Tretchikoff art classic, 'Blue Lady', above a tiny fireplace and created a quirky side table from a Fifties coloured chair, where a mis-matched floral light sits on it like a sculpture (*above*).

soft natural The living room of Nadia Yaron and Myriah Scruggs is eclectic, yet carefully thrown together. Their decoration is rough around the edges. An old cloth haphazardly covers the sofa, while the paintwork is loose and carefree. Large plants in giant pots bring the outdoors inside. Instead of curtains, their windows are covered with antique shutters and soft gauzy muslins to make the most of the light (*opposite page*).

neutral chic The colour scheme in Nadia and Myriah's home exudes quiet, calm tones of creams, browns, whites, taupes and sand. The wooden floor boasts its original patina, which works well with the earthy, natural palette. A wonderful mix of natural, organic textiles – linens, cottons, hemp, calicos and jutes – create a soft, comforting feel to this living room. They've created many nooks and crannies to relax, like the built-in day bed (*above*), sited right next to a tall window, and the chaise longue, softened with a mattress and a thick, striped rug (*left*). The duo have used textiles to create a whimsical feel, with antique cloths draped over an old wooden ladder and a sheet of muslin suspended from the ceiling. Another length of muslin draped over a pole covers the window, letting in the sun's warming rays, but keeping a sense of privacy.

modern comforts Shop owner David Alhadeff mixes classics together in this completely unique living room. An old, handsome Chesterfield sofa looks masculine against the round contours of the delicate Eames rocking chair, softened with a white sheepskin. Cushions soften the overall look while a large rug delineates the living space. The quirky deer adds a little humour (*above*).

powerful pink In this corner (*left*), David has covered an Eames sofa with a funky fabric and contrasted it against a hot pink wall. Instead of wall art, his hipster hat collection creates an iconic feature. David has a penchant for porcelain pets, like the bulldog (*above*) and the cat, curled up on the sofa (*left*).

nooks for books

In the living room of Cécile
Daladier and Nicolas Soulier
in Paris (*previous pages*), modern
and vintage work side by side.
Two classic fold out 'Butterfly
chairs', originally conceived by
Jorge Ferrari-Hardoy in 1939,
sit alongside a huge glass-topped
coffee table. With thin, model
legs, the table looks like it is
floating; the glass top reflects
the light into the living room.
The floor-to-ceiling book shelf is
the room's most striking feature,
packed with old magazines, coffee
table books and collections of
glassware, toys and other items.

old glamour

Here, an old lamp makes a
gorgeous centrepiece in Claire
Basler's elegant room. While the
scheme is dark and moody, the
large windows are reflected in
the tall mirrors, creating a sense
of space (*left*).

creature comforts In Tim Rundle's living room (*above*), the colour scheme is strictly soft pistachios, yellow, white and black. Vintage pieces ground this contemporary living room. In the corner, a collection of antique bottles, souvenirs, photos and vases create a dense, rich area of visual interest (*see left for detail*). The glamorous gold-yellow chandelier is in fact made of plastic, bought over from Italy in the bottom of a rucksack. Against the backdrop of a grey suedette Seventies-style suite, a mix of cushion shapes and styles stand out. On the table is an African-inspired sculpture of a baobab tree and two cheeky English squirrels, plotting world domination.

natural comforts In the living room of Kristin Norris and Trevor Lunn, modern wooden birds swoop down from the ceiling. A natural rug covers the wooden floor, creating a warm, comfortable area. Textiles, like the blanket on the back of the chair and the large cushions, provide a welcoming feel (*right*).

luxe modern In the sitting room of Nina Tolstrup and Jack Mama, classic modern pieces and the handmade mix together to create a comfortable space. An old Eames moulded plywood chair sits amongst other classics, while a collection of wooden wall clocks keeps the natural feel going. This low-level coffee table doubles up as a magazine storage space (*below*).

flower power In these two rooms, nature reigns supreme. In Ann Shore's London apartment, floral paintings, postcards, tiles, faux flowers, dainty duvets, cushions and posters bring in beautiful blooms everywhere. She has created an informal table by placing an old door on top of tall cardboard boxes (*above*). In France, artist Claire Basler fills her studio with huge blooms, like these cuttings of irises, mimosa and peonies, which reflect her generous-sized canvases. Antique radiators give warmth to this large space in the winter, while a huge lampshade and a modern plastic mushroom-shaped sidelight create eclectic lighting features (*opposite page*).

city nomad In Ann Shore's living room, life appears simple, like a space for an urban nomad: things feel like they could be packed up in a heartbeat. With her amazing view of East London, the floor-to-ceiling windows create a stunning backdrop; a vast vista is spread out before anyone perched on the corner pouffe. A fold-out cane deckchair, a soft rug and a cushion make casual seating. The wooden floor reflects the light around the room, making the space feel natural and earthy. Big wooden bowls with *objets trouvés* also make the room feel casual, like they'd just been bought in from an expedition outdoors. A mirror is gently reclining against a bare wall, again making the room feel somehow impermanent (*above*).

urban picnic On Ann Shore's balcony, you'd hardly think you were in the heart of urban London. A heavy wooden table with benches – adorned with a delicate lace tablecloth and foxglove flowers in a milk jug – awaits food and guests. To make the area feel private, she has created a natural screen with large plants in chunky pots.

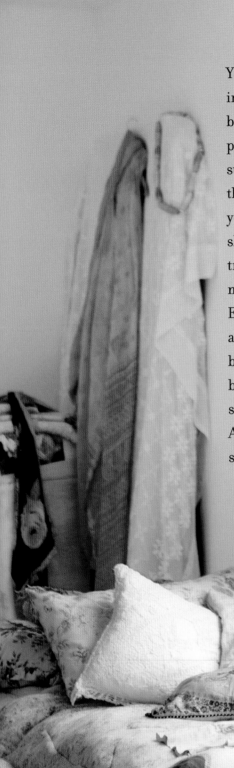

You'll sleep soundly
in a modern vintage
bedroom. In a quiet,
peaceful room,
surrounded by all
the things you love,
you'll be able to
slumber with old
treasures and
modern pleasures.
Enjoy the texture of
antique linen sheets,
but with the hi-tech
beauty of a pocket-
sprung mattress.
And of course, it all
starts with the bed…

The star of the bedroom is the bed itself. When choosing a model, think about the frame and how it could be worked into modern vintage style. Choose a contemporary four-poster and throw over antique linens or cherry-pick an old wooden bed and dress it with modern graphic prints. The key is to clash styles. Look for four-poster beds, sleigh beds, or wrought-iron frames. If you find a piece with a heavenly shape, but questionable colour, create contrast by painting it in a funky hue, like a zesty green or bright yellow. For a clean, fresh look, a bright white makes all styles feel contemporary again.

Like every book has its cover, so has every bed. In a modern vintage setting, some of the textiles you'll see are simply artworks. Scour second-hand shops for hand-woven linens, painstakingly hand-stitched patchwork quilts, or old paisley duvets. Throw on unusual pieces, like pashmina scarves or thick woollen army blankets, or create your own throw: reclaim old retro curtains and roll-ends of vintage fabrics and sew them together, boldly clashing pattern and colour. For sheets, create contrast with an unexpected color like bright green, pale orange or turquoise to make them feel fresh again.

Adorn your backdrop with a mélange of cushions with funky, contrasting prints. Pair different shades, periods and fabric textures; juxtapose crochet cushions against patchwork, or graphic prints against stripes. Again, this clash of styles creates vibrancy and pockets of colour. Pairing any colour with white will provide a crisp, classic contrast. Try and keep to a bed that has half a dozen carefully chosen pillows. Mix up styles like flange, knife-edge or ruffle pillows in solid colours, throwing in a patterned pillow to add a twist.

For a unique bedside table, search antique shops for items like empty barrels, ornate chairs, small drawer units or simply stack up a collection of old suitcases. Otherwise, pile up magazines, antique hatboxes, or wicker hamper baskets for an impromptu surface.

For most of us, our bedroom doubles up as a dressing room, so clothes storage matters. We need to keep our clothes accessible and yet, to keep a room tranquil, these clothes need to be tidied away out of sight. To house your precious garb, keep your eye out for old wardrobes. With many people choosing built-in storage, a lot of these grand old pieces end up on street corners looking for a home. Some will need a little restoration, yet there's nothing paint or even a strip of wallpaper can't do. Make sure your ceiling is high enough, however, so the rest of the room won't feel dwarfed by this imposing feature. You can always remove the doors and expose the storage space inside or replace big fusty doors with curtains of retro cloth or old linen. Alternatively, try an open-style hanging system and put some of your clothing on show, like a collection of hats, jewellery or bags, hung from pretty, padded vintage

perchance to dream Cherry-pick vintage pieces and mix them up with modern comforts. Sandrine Place's bedroom mixes a strictly modern table with a classic lamp, while the bed is covered in antique fabrics (*above*). At Derrière, a hi-tech stereo is mounted to a chipped and peeling wall and a mirrored ceiling clashes with the original parquet floors below (*opposite*).

hangers or classic curvaceous coat stands.

With drawers, you'll always find standard high street pieces, but think laterally about using other units, like old industrial or ex-office drawers. Again, you can easily customize any period with a new colour or paper. If you do choose something ordinary, make it extraordinary by choosing an art nouveau or a round Sixties mirror to perch on top. For more of a vintage look, store your jumpers or extra rugs in old tea chests, antique suitcases or Far Eastern-style trunks.

Every bedroom needs a thoughtful mix of lighting. Most of us like to read in bed so a sidelight is a key piece. Retro print fabrics stretched over a lampshade frame look pretty when lit, and striking clashed with a modern, masculine base. Add interest to a traditional room with an offbeat industrial bedside lamp or a strictly modern floor lamp. Crowning the room is often a pendant light, so add a bit of glamour with a chandelier, create softness with a round paper shade or go wild with a bold, colourful, retro fabric lampshade. Whatever you do, make it a show-stopper.

At night, you'll want window coverings to shut out any street lights, while by day, you'll want to let in the sun's rays, but perhaps not prying eyes. For total blackout, traditional shutters work well with a modern vintage look, while thick curtains from reclaimed retro fabrics inject colour and character. There's nothing like antique lace or a loose linen weave to allow a soft, diffused light to gently wake you when the sun rises.

For walls, either choose something neutral to place your modern vintage pictures on, or go for colour. Pick out any hue you can sleep with;

a soft olive green, a dark mushroom or a quiet black. The bedroom is one place that can take a lot of pattern, so add strips of old vintage wallpaper to one wall, but be careful not to create visual overload.

Feet need to be greeted with something soft when you wake, so choose a warm floor covering. Wood always feels welcoming underfoot. Otherwise, cloak your floors with an assortment of rugs. Particularly if you have plain walls, mix and match floor coverings for a clash of styles. Equally, Persian rugs and sheep and cow skins are timeless classics, and so fit with both modern and vintage looks.

Most rooms need a place to sit, but pick wisely. Contrast looks, so consider a Sixties bubble chair in a traditional room or an elegant French chair in a modern room.

Since bedrooms are intimate, personal places, display a few of your favourite things: create spaces where you can show the things that make you happy. Put postcards, photos and paintings on display in clusters. A piece of vintage artwork on the wall, like an iconic painting of a scene from a different era or a group of sepia toned photographs, evokes a sense of nostalgia for a bygone time. Or, if you have a modern artwork, juxtapose it with a vintage frame or vice versa.

And sleep well.

back to black Against a black backdrop, the pieces in the London home of James Russell and Hannah Plumb look simply stunning. The portraits on the wall evoke a sense of history, along with the old linen sheet and bright green floral bedspread. The bedhead looks handsome in its raw, unpainted wooden state. The patina of old wood brings in a feeling of natural warmth to the room. Wake up fresh in the morning to colourful, scented wildflowers, like the pretty stems seen here, arranged in a collection of glass vessels (*right*).

mix and match A wrought-iron bedstead gives gives Dean Sawyer's bedroom a vintage feel, along with the bijou wooden side table, topped with a modernist lamp. On top, a mis-match of textiles gives the bed a welcoming feel, while beside the bed, a striped rug makes a warm welcome underfoot in the morning (*above*). At the foot of the bed (*right*), a utility cabinet has been painted, polished and given legs to create a display space for memorabilia. Beside it, a small chair provides a space to dress.

layer, layer Artist Claire Basler's bedroom perfectly sums up modern vintage. The bed is by IKEA, and yet she sleeps in the finest vintage French linen sheets, all embroidered and initialled by hand. Beside it are skyscrapers of flowers, arranged in tall, elegant contemporary vases. Claire brings nature, her inspiration, inside whenever she can, which is why she's painted the stunning woodland canvas behind her bed (*above*).

nest In French artist Nathalie Lete's Parisian bedroom, a mix of textiles adds comfort. Two thick floral rugs provide warmth to her wooden floor, while her bed is adorned with a cluster of colourful, round, crocheted cushions. As her ceiling is high, a grand wooden wardrobe looks right at home, providing storage space for clothes. She mixes lighting, with an industrial sidelight on one side and a soft fabric-covered lamp on the other (*right*).

quiet haven In the Nottingham home of Tim Rundle, the bedroom is on the top floor – a peaceful haven. His favourite colours, soft blues, yellows, pale greens and whites mix together with dark browns and blacks. Tim is master of the eclectic: on the top of a linen cupboard, there's a deer and several vintage vases, while a unique artwork, created entirely from feathers, sits on the floor. A comfortable armchair, part of the sofa set seen in the living room, makes a relaxing place to sit (*above*). On the generously large bed, embroidered blue and white pillows add a feminine touch, while the light blue bedspread adds extra warmth. Behind the floor-to-ceiling curtains, are the couple's clothes, cleverly hidden from view. On the other side of the room, a similar size and hued curtain covers the windows, creating a sense of symmetry. The sculptural lamp, seen behind the bed, was a find in a local import shop. For the ultimate underfoot comfort, cream carpet covers the entire floor (*right*).

bedside beauty Beside Ann Shore's bed in London, she's fashioned her own bedside table from sturdy cardboard storage covered with inspirational pictures, to create a montage of special images and colours. On top, Ann has clustered an assortment of all things found. She has collected shells, jewellery boxes and trinkets to create a personal treasure trove.

luxe lace In Ann's bedroom, swathes of lace grace the windows and bed, making a soft, whimsical space that's beautiful to behold. Delicate layered material over the windows mean she'll wake up naturally with the daylight. Ann has covered her bed with lace pillows and more layered pieces of lace to add prettiness to a plain white duvet. Wicker baskets and old wooden drawers provide storage, while a candle sits on top just waiting to be lit. Ann drapes her necklaces, hats and flower garlands to decorate the walls. A string of seashells also evokes a sense of holidays and places far, far away from the bustling London crowd.

floral medley

In Petra Boase's guest room (*opposite page*), a medley of fabrics covers the bed. Florals mix with a patchwork quilt, a pretty duvet and a striped valance. The pendant and side light match, providing visual symmetry in a room of clashing patterns all based around a colour scheme of yellow, pink, green and blue.

patchwork fantastic

French artist Nathalie Lete has painted pictures of birds, butterflies and dragonflies in a gorgeous mural (*above*). She creates her own soft toy creatures, seen beside and on her bed, and has made a stunning patchwork quilt out of old fabric, placing cushions on top to create a pillow patchwork, too.

knit wit

In her typical, whimsical way, Aurelie Mathigot has stitched her own patchwork quilt, the pretty white lampshade and the funky knitted tea set on top of elegant drawers (*right*).

memories In Nathalie Lete's bedroom (*right*), she successfully contrasts modern and vintage pieces. Beside her bed, on top of an old side table, is a birdcage with decorative model birds, while an industrial lamp sits on top. She's created the lamp on the other side by matching a quirky fabric lampshade to a flower-covered base. For the walls, she's used a fresh green contrasted with white to bring in a vibrant feel and create a plain canvas to showcase her most beloved objects in a patch of collected treasures (*detailed below*). Love hearts, Buddha eyes, jewellery and miniature art create an ornate pocket of detail.

soft green In Kristin Norris and Trevor Lunn's bedroom (*above*), the backdrop is a gentle teal green — a soft soothing colour. They have left the walls mostly uncluttered to provide a relaxing place, free of visual noise. To be kind to sleepy feet and to soften the wooden floors, they've laid out a large graphic rug. An old rickety fan rests on top of a plastic side table, while an industrial-style work lamp provides bedside lighting. On the bed, a mix of fabrics — natural felted wool, linen and silk — makes a nest for sleepers.

pattern frenzy

In Petra Boase's Norfolk home (*left*), she's gone pattern-tastic. With so many textiles, the overall effect feels homely and comforting, perhaps because many of the pieces she's chosen are labours of love, like the crocheted valance, or the patchwork quilt and cushions. On the floor, she's kept the pattern theme going with a brightly coloured rug, while the floral curtain simply seems like a fabric continuation of the stripes of vintage wallpaper. One of Petra's playful 'love' pictures is on the wall, her own artistic touch. In another bedroom (*above*) she's also used a clash of pattern, with a floral theme underpinning the room: tropical blooms, rose heads and the tiny flower patterns on the wallpaper work together to provide visual symmetry. Small patches of plain colour, like the white sheets and the lampshade bases, provide contrast to the pattern around them. She's employed a modern, Eames-style coat rack for her collection of scarves and bags (*right*).

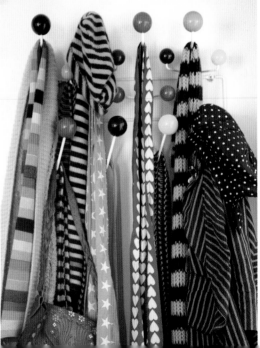

pink and pretty In Nathalie Lete's daughter's attic bedroom (*below*), there's a mixture of pink, white and pattern. Plenty of textiles make it feel soft and welcoming. A line of bunting stretches across the room, while two colourful rugs provide extra comfort on the carpeted floor. Natalie has painted a mural of flowers and butterflies directly across the wall and radiator. She has left the room's largest canvases, the roof and the wall, in white, but she's painted the exposed beams in hot pink.

girl power In another view of Nathalie's daughter's room (*above*), she's mixed up different shades of pink, painting her shelf storage in a soft pink, while a striking hot pink rug covers the floor. Nathalie has fashioned the perfect seating area, with plenty of patchwork and funky, fluffy cushions and an oversized teddy bear for extra comfort. With such a huge rug – her own design – and plenty of seating, this makes the perfect den to have a tea party with friends.

boy power Her son's room (*right*) is painted in masculine black, yet she's used pockets of pattern, such as the hand-crocheted covers, to bring in a sense of homeliness and vibrancy. The room is a boy's haven, with globe pendant lights hanging from the ceiling, a pirate's flag, a light-up moon and a skeleton hanging on the wall. A large Union Jack also brings in strong colour. Two favourite toys, a dog and a bear, look like they've found their own perfect place to retire.

bathe

There's nothing quite like slipping into the warm, scented water of your own private oasis. Statistics show we spend three years of our life bathing, so investing some thought in the bathroom is well worth it. Bathrooms are our own private spaces, where we relax, wash and get ready to face the world or bid the day goodnight. Modern vintage bathrooms blend the best of contemporary conveniences with the beautiful classics the past has given us. The result is very, very relaxing.

Modern life has given us the mod-cons that make a bathroom comfortable, yet it's the old things, like the feel of a big brass tap/faucet, a sofa-sized bathtub, or the deluge of water that rains on you from a large Victorian rosehead, which can make them truly luxurious.

When it comes to designing your modern vintage bathroom, again it's about contrast. Choose vintage or reproduction centrepieces (bathtub, toilet, sink) to suit a fresh modern setting, or make your centrepieces chic and sleek, accessorizing with traditional wall and floor finishes, or vintage textile accessories.

One of your investment buys will be your bathtub (although if you're sourcing these from salvage shops, they don't need to be expensive). Whatever the era, no tub design is as classic as the freestanding clawfoot. Luxurious and practical, these pieces always look elegant and sophisticated. Styles such as slipper and double slipper tubs (where one end or both are raised) offer a truly glamorous vintage look and if you put the taps/faucets in the middle,

it makes a comfortable bath for two. For a modern twist, you can paint or paper the outside of the bath in a fresh colour, or if the claw feet need replacing, choose something modern, like sleek stainless steel or big hunks of dark timber as a plinth for the tub. The pedestal bathtub, which sits on a short base, is perfect for modern vintage bathrooms, and you can find them in a variety of materials, including cast-iron and old-fashioned copper. If you already have a modern bath, consider accessorizing with traditional fittings. If you're lucky, you'll find Victorian brass taps/faucets at car boot sales, or look out for modern reproductions of classic, shapely designs.

If you've gone traditional with your bath, perhaps pick a sleek modern sink to contrast. Otherwise, consider a console sink, which can either be freestanding (with four long legs) or attached to the wall (with two legs). You'll find a variety of styles, with bases in different materials, like wood and porcelain. To achieve a modern vintage look, try painting the base in a striking colour or choose industrial-style legs for your old-fashioned sink top.

Even toilets can have a vintage twist. Look out for old-fashioned pull chain toilets, and accessorize with quirky handles (you could fashion one yourself from beads or an old stop-watch) and toilet roll holders.

When it comes to walls and floors, there's nothing quite like tiles. Slate mosaic tiles were used in Victorian times, while small mosaic tiles are more modern on splashback areas. Underfoot, it's hard to beat the traditional black and white tiled floor or sandstone antique finished tiles. Granite and marble also recreate a classic look. Linoleum, now

instant elegance Petra Boase's bathroom is bijou, but at the same time serene. The collection of swans, seen above the shelves, on the toilet cistern and in the picture below, bring in a sense of elegance and grace (*above*). Add instant glamour to a bathroom just by adding a single candle sconce, as have James Russell and Hannah Plumb (*opposite*). Simple touches like these don't take a lot of effort to transform the ordinary into the extraordinary.

back in fashion and available in a huge array of hues, harks back to Victorian times and is incredibly practical in bathrooms.

Heating is very important in bathrooms and nothing beats a generously sized, old-fashioned radiator. Equally, there are some striking contemporary radiators in an array of shapes. Contrast with your overall look.

Every bathroom needs well thought out lighting. Sconce lighting is traditional in bathrooms and comes in a variety of styles, from modern cubist to art nouveau and contemporary. If your room is small, dot light fixtures around the perimeter of the ceiling to create a sense of space, but see if you can install a dimmer switch so the lighting isn't too stark. Otherwise, low pendant lights with modern or retro shades add a touch of class and glamour. But be practical and add a decent, modern vanity light near the sink mirror.

The mirror above the sink is usually in a prominent position, so choose wisely. Select something quirky and original and your whole bathroom will somehow feel more inviting. Keep your eye out for a glamorous gilt-edged framed mirror or something from the Twenties, with an art deco twist, or create a striking montage of mirrors from different eras. Otherwise, a collection of old-fashioned hand-held mirrors will create a unique look. If your bathroom is erring more to the traditional side, a large modern mirror can pull it back from looking too fusty.

An easy way to throw vintage into your modern bathroom is to accessorize with towels, bathmats and curtains. When you're shopping, look out for monogrammed or graphic towels, reproduction towels in vintage prints, bobbled

bathmats and other pieces. Many shower curtains come in reproduction vintage prints.

Since many bathrooms are small, good storage is key. On walls, you can secure old medicine cabinets, glass fronted cupboards or open shelving to display your quirky finds. A little nature works well here, so display sea sponges, conch shells or pot plants. Porcelain swans, wooden dolphins or shapely perfume bottles also create little areas of gorgeousness.

Other details, like Victorian soap dishes, china toothbrush holders or wicker toilet roll holders also give that vintage feel. Victorian porcelain washing bowls and jugs also add a sense of faded glamour, along with vintage robe hooks and old trunks for your towels.

eclectic glamour

eclectic glamour Transform a functional, everyday piece, like this hand-washing basin, into the extraordinary. Pebbles make an unusual splashback to the stone basin, bringing in a natural seaside vibe. The big mirror above reflects light into the small space, while the hanging mirror, adorned with a necklace, is there more for its handsome frame and good looks. Of course, there's nothing like a chandelier in the bathroom to add instant glamour (*above*). The bathroom in Derrière, a restaurant in Paris, has been transformed into something far from the ordinary with playful tiles, original lighting and patterned metallic paper. A collection of old mirrors all in similar shapes and sizes, creates a sense of space by reflecting light into an otherwise petite room (*right*). To keep the restaurant's mantra of being 'a home away from home', the designers, the Mazouz brothers, have instilled a modern vintage feel with antique floor tiles laid in an eccentric, modern way (*far right*).

old world comforts

In Claire Basler's bathroom, she has
a generously-sized vintage claw foot
bathtub. Her trademark giant floral
paintings, in this case irises on a silver
canvas, provide a beautiful backdrop
to bathe by. Linen towels hang from
an old towel rail, heated by a shapely
antique radiator (*opposite page*). Her
sink is flanked by two low-hanging
modern pendant lights, providing
useful lighting for washing rituals.
A practical row of contemporary
IKEA bathroom cabinets runs along
the wall (*this page*).

reincarnate key pieces

An elegant, modern, square-legged side table becomes a practical bathing aid in Tim Rundle's bathroom. On top, a vintage silver jug and soap dish reside, adding glinting, pretty accessories. Here, tiles play with proportion: large square floor tiles juxtapose with the tiny taupe and white mosaic tiles on the walls. The bath, painted in taupe, continues the natural, neutral feel. The large floor-to-ceiling window brings in the natural world, making this the perfect urban space to relax and reflect (*opposite page*).

neutral love In Nadia Yaron and Myriah Scruggs' bathroom, as in the rest of their home, the backdrop is of quiet, sedate neutrals, with their trademark salvaged furniture and fabrics. In this case, the bath curtain has been hand-sewn from rough-but-pretty linen (*above*), while the neutral paint has rough edges, making the white ceiling 'lift' so the room seems more generously portioned. A glamorous floor lamp, found on Craig's List and acquired for just a few dollars, transforms the whole room (*right*).

sources

Modern vintage style is more of an approach than a look. Giving vintage a modern twist provides plenty of shopping opportunities at home and away.

Whether you're looking for inspiration or to extend your existing collections, seek out old-fashioned jumble sales, garage sales and car-boot sales. Smaller local markets often have bric-à-brac stalls, as do church, village and school fêtes. Visit local antique shops, charity shops, auctions and architectural salvage yards. Keep your eyes open for interesting-looking skips.

Continue the modern vintage search on holiday – if you are in France, locate the nearest brocante, often housed in a church or village hall.

Surf the internet for larger antique and collectors' markets, national and international. You might want to plan travel-time to coincide with yearly European or American fairs.

The web also hosts a wealth of antique and auctioneering sites, providing plenty of opportunities for international purchases. Here are a few sources to get you started:

IN THE UK

MODERN VINTAGE SHOPPING

Baileys Home and Garden
Whitecross Farm
Bridstow
Herefordshire
HR9 6JU
Tel: +44 (0)1989 561931
www.baileyshomeandgarden.com
Eat drink and shop modern vintage. The Baileys have created the perfect day out.

Caravan
3 Redchurch Street
London
E2 7DJ
Tel: +44 (0)20 7033 3532
www.caravanstyle.com
Interior stylist and author Emily Chalmers handpicks a decorative selection for the modern vintage-inspired home.

Visit caravanstyle.com to click through to British artist Deborah Bowness' catalogue of witty hand-printed trompe l'oeil wallpaper featuring panels of vintage frocks, standard lamps and busy bookshelves.

Labour and Wait
85 Redchurch Street
London
E2 7DJ
Tel: +44 (0)20 7729 6253
www.labourandwait.co.uk
Vintage inspired hardware with a modern twist.

Liberty
Great Marlborough Street
London
W1B 5AH
Tel: +44 (0)20 7734 1234
www.liberty.co.uk
Floors of fabrics, furniture lighting and textiles. Modern and vintage.

Moth
154 Burton Road
West Didsbury
Manchester
M20 1IH
Tel: +44 (0)161 445 9847
www.mothstyle.com
Inspiring home decoration, accessories and gifts – all carefully curated by interior stylist Hazel Marchant.

Pimpernel & Partners
596 Kings Road
London
SW6 2DX
Tel: +44 (0)20 7731 2448
www.pimpernelandpartners.co.uk
A lovely vintage selection partnered with calico covered upholstery.

Story
The Old Truman Brewery
4–5 Dray Walk
London
E1 6QL
Tel: +44 (0)20 7246 3137
www.storydeli.com
Treat yourself to an organic pizza then browse the modern vintage offering from creative Ann Shore, both under the same roof – perfect!

ARCHITECTURAL ANTIQUES AND SALVAGE

Lassco
www.lassco.co.uk
Architectural salvage in London and Oxfordshire.

Retrouvious
www.retrouvious.com
London-based architectural salvage company. Cherry-pick one-off items or fit out a whole house. Design projects also undertaken.

Salvoweb
www.salvoweb.com
Online directory of architectural salvage suppliers, antiques, and reclaimed materials.

ANTIQUE AND FLEA MARKETS
Among regular UK antique fairs are those at Newark (Notts), Swinderby (Lincs), Ardingly (East Sussex) and Goodwood (West Sussex). See www.antiques-atlas.com and www.artefact.co.uk for more information.

If you're up for jumping on the Eurostar to see what Paris has to offer, visit www.parispuces.com.

For general information on street markets in London, visit www.londonmarkets.co.uk. Consult individual websites below for specific days and seasonal opening hours.

Brick Lane
Brick Lane, Cheshire Street and
Sclater Street, London E1 and E2
www.londonmarkets.com

Bermondsey
Bermondsey Square, Southwark, London SE1
www.bermondseysquare.co.uk/antiques

Camden
Camden High Street, London NW1
www.camdenlock.net

Greenwich
Greenwich Church Street, Stockwell Street and Greenwich High Road, London SE10
www.greenwich-market.co.uk

Portobello
Portobello Road, London W11
www.portobelloroad.co.uk

IN THE USA

MODERN VINTAGE SHOPPING

Anthropologie
www.anthropologie.com
Stores across North America and Canada. Now in the UK too!

ABC Carpet and Home
www.abchome.com
Stores in Manhattan, the Bronx, New Jersey and Florida.

Restoration Hardware
www.restorationhardware.com
Stores across the US.

ANTIQUE AND FLEA MARKETS
The USA hosts a wealth of modern vintage outlets in the form of thrift stores and markets. Check websites for locations and dates.

For comprehensive state-by-state flea-market directories, visit www.fleausa.com and www.fleamarketguide.com.

California
Rose Bowl Flea Market
www.rgcshows.com

Massachusetts
Brimfield Antiques Show
www.brimfieldshow.com

New Jersey
Englishtown Auction Sales
www.englishtownauction.com

New York
Hell's Kitchen Flea Market
www.hellskitchenfleamarket.com

For indispensable flea market inspiration, visit Mary Randolph Carter Berg's site for the flea market devotee at www.carterjunk.com.

credits

KEY: **a** = above, **b** = below, **r** = right, **l** = left, **c** = centre, **in** = inset

Endpapers The London home of Creative Ann Shore of Story; **1** Home of Tim Rundle and Glynn Jones; **2** The restaurant 'Derrière' designed and owned by the 'Mazouz Brothers'; **3in** and **4in** The home of artist Claire Basler in France; **5a** The home of Kristin Norris and Trevor Lunn, Philadelphia; **5c** Dean Sawyer and Steve Drum; **5b** The home of Nadia Yaron and Myriah Scruggs of Nightwood in Brooklyn; **7al** The home of artist Claire Basler in France; **7ar** The London home of Creative Ann Shore of Story; **7bl** The restaurant 'Derrière' designed and owned by the 'Mazouz Brothers'; **7br** The home of James Russell & Hannah Plumb, the artists behind JamesPlumb www.Jamesplumb.co.uk; **8–9** The home of artist Claire Basler in France; **12** The home of Nadia Yaron and Myriah Scruggs of Nightwood in Brooklyn; **14in** The home and studio of the art & craft artist Nathalie Lete in Paris; **15** The home of Nadia Yaron and Myriah Scruggs of Nightwood in Brooklyn; **16–19** Home of Tim Rundle and Glynn Jones; **20** The Norfolk family home of the designer Petra Boase; **21** The home of Kristin Norris and Trevor Lunn, Philadelphia; **22** The home of artist Claire Basler in France; **23a** The French home of the interior stylist and consultant Sandrine Place; **23b** The home of James Russell & Hannah Plumb, the artists behind JamesPlumb www.Jamesplumb.co.uk; **24al** and **bl** Home of Tim Rundle and Glynn Jones; **24r** and **25** The family home of Nina Tolstrup and Jack Mama of www.studiomama.com; **26** and **28in** The restaurant 'Derrière' designed and owned by the 'Mazouz Brothers'; **29in** The home of Nadia Yaron and Myriah Scruggs of Nightwood in Brooklyn; **30al** www.aureliemathigot.com; **30ar** The Norfolk family home of the designer Petra Boase; **30bl** Home of Tim Rundle and Glynn Jones; **30br** www.aureliemathigot.com; **31** The French home of the interior stylist and consultant Sandrine Place; **32** Home of Tim Rundle and Glynn Jones; **33al** The London home of Creative Ann Shore of Story; **33 ar in** The restaurant 'Derrière' designed and owned by the 'Mazouz Brothers'; **33br** www.dearswallow.com; **34al** The home of Kristin Norris and Trevor Lunn, Philadelphia; **34ac** and **bl** The French home of the interior stylist and consultant Sandrine Place; **34ar** The home of James Russell & Hannah Plumb, the artists behind JamesPlumb www.Jamesplumb.co.uk; **34bc** Home of Tim Rundle and Glynn Jones; **34br** www.dearswallow.com; **35** The home of Kristin Norris and Trevor Lunn, Philadelphia; **36** The London home of Creative Ann Shore of Story; **38in** The home and studio of the art & craft artist Nathalie Lete in Paris; **39r** www.aureliemathigot.com; **40al** Dean Sawyer and Steve Drum; **40ar** The home and studio of the art & craft artist Nathalie Lete in Paris; **40bl** The French home of the interior stylist and consultant Sandrine Place; **40br** and **41** The Norfolk family home of the designer Petra Boase; **42–43** www.aureliemathigot.com; **44–45** The Norfolk family home of the designer Petra Boase; **46** The home of Kristin Norris and Trevor Lunn, Philadelphia; **47al** and **r** The home of Nadia Yaron and Myriah Scruggs of Nightwood in Brooklyn; **47bl** Dean Sawyer and Steve Drum; **48** The home of artist Claire Basler in France; **50** www.aureliemathigot.com; **51** The home of David Alhadeff, owner of The Future Perfect; **52** The home of artist Claire Basler in France; **53** The home of Nadia Yaron and Myriah Scruggs of Nightwood in Brooklyn; **54** The home of artist Claire Basler in France; **55l** The home of Kristin Norris and Trevor Lunn, Philadelphia; **55r** The home of David Alhadeff, owner of The Future Perfect; **56 background** The restaurant 'Derrière' designed and owned by the 'Mazouz Brothers'; **56a in** The Norfolk family home of the designer Petra Boase; **56b in** Home of Tim Rundle and Glynn Jones; **57** The home of David Alhadeff, owner of The Future Perfect; **58al** and **ac** www.aureliemathigot.com; **58ar** The restaurant 'Derrière' designed and owned by the 'Mazouz Brothers'; **58bl** Dean Sawyer and Steve Drum; **58bc**

and **59** www.aureliemathigot.com; **58br** The home of David Alhadeff, owner of The Future Perfect; **60** The London home of Creative Ann Shore of Story; **62in** The home of Kristin Norris and Trevor Lunn, Philadelphia; **63in** www.dearswallow.com; **64–65** The London home of Creative Ann Shore of Story; **66a** The home and studio of the art & craft artist Nathalie Lete in Paris; **66bl** and **br** The home of Kristin Norris and Trevor Lunn, Philadelphia; **67l** The home of James Russell & Hannah Plumb, the artists behind JamesPlumb www.Jamesplumb.co.uk; **67r** The home of Nadia Yaron and Myriah Scruggs of Nightwood in Brooklyn; **68** The home and studio of the art & craft artist Nathalie Lete in Paris; **69al, ar** and **c** www.dearswallow.com; **69ac** Home of Tim Rundle and Glynn Jones; **69bl** The restaurant 'Derrière' designed and owned by the 'Mazouz Brothers'; **69br** The French home of the interior stylist and consultant Sandrine Place; **70l** www.dearswallow.com; **70ar** The home of James Russell & Hannah Plumb, the artists behind JamesPlumb www.Jamesplumb.co.uk; **70br** and **71** The home of artist Claire Basler in France; **72a** The family home of Nina Tolstrup and Jack Mama of www.studiomama.com; **72b** The restaurant 'Derrière' designed and owned by the 'Mazouz Brothers'; **73** The home of artist Claire Basler in France; **74** and **75al** The home and studio of the art & craft artist Nathalie Lete in Paris; **75ar** www.aureliemathigot.com; **75b** The Norfolk family home of the designer Petra Boase; **78** The home of artist Claire Basler in France; **79** The home of James Russell & Hannah Plumb, the artists behind JamesPlumb www.Jamesplumb.co.uk; **80in** Dean Sawyer and Steve Drum; **81in** The home of Kristin Norris and Trevor Lunn, Philadelphia; **82** www.aureliemathigot.com; **83** The home of Kristin Norris and Trevor Lunn, Philadelphia; **84–85** Home of Tim Rundle and Glynn Jones; **86–87** The London home of Creative Ann Shore of Story; **88a** The home of David Alhadeff, owner of The Future Perfect; **88b** The family home of Nina Tolstrup and Jack Mama of www.studiomama.com; **89** The house of Assaï in Paris; **90a** and **br** Dean Sawyer and Steve Drum; **90bl** The house of Assaï in Paris; **91** Dean Sawyer and Steve Drum; **92–93** The Norfolk family home of the designer Petra Boase; **94–95** The home of artist Claire Basler in France; **96** The restaurant 'Derrière' designed and owned by the 'Mazouz Brothers'; **97l** The home of James Russell & Hannah Plumb, the artists behind JamesPlumb www.jamesplumb.co.uk; **97r** The French home of the interior stylist and consultant Sandrine Place; **98–99** The home of artist Claire Basler in France; **101** Dean Sawyer and Steve Drum; **102** and **103a** www.dearswallow.com; **103b** The restaurant 'Derrière' designed and owned by the 'Mazouz Brothers'; **104** The home of Kristin Norris and Trevor Lunn, Philadelphia; **105** The house of Assaï in Paris; **106–107** The home of artist Claire Basler in France; **108** The French home of the interior stylist and consultant Sandrine Place; **109** The London home of Creative Ann Shore of Story; **110–111** The Norfolk family home of the designer Petra Boase; **112–113** The home of Nadia Yaron and Myriah Scruggs of Nightwood in Brooklyn; **114–115** The house of Assaï in Paris; **116** The home of David Alhadeff, owner of The Future Perfect; **117** The home of artist Claire Basler in France; **118** Home of Tim Rundle and Glynn Jones; **119a** The home of Kristin Norris and Trevor Lunn, Philadelphia; **119b** The family home of Nina Tolstrup and Jack Mama of www.studiomama.com; **120** The London home of Creative Ann Shore of Story; **121** The home of artist Claire Basler in France; **122–125** The London home of Creative Ann Shore of Story; **126in** The French home of the interior stylist and consultant Sandrine Place; **127** The restaurant 'Derrière' designed and owned by the 'Mazouz Brothers'; **128** Dean Sawyer and Steve Drum; **129** The home of James Russell & Hannah Plumb, the artists behind JAMESPLUMB www.jamesplumb.co.uk; **130–131** The home of artist Claire Basler in France; **131r** The home and studio of the art & craft artist Nathalie Lete in Paris; **132–133** Home of Tim Rundle and Glynn Jones; **134–135** The

London home of Creative Ann Shore of Story; **136** The Norfolk family home of the designer Petra Boase; **137a** The home and studio of the art & craft artist Nathalie Lete in Paris; **137b** www.aureliemathigot.com; **138a** The home of Kristin Norris and Trevor Lunn, Philadelphia; **138b** and **139** The home and studio of the art & craft artist Nathalie Lete in Paris; **140–141** The Norfolk family home of the designer Petra Boase; **142–143** The home and studio of the art & craft artist Nathalie Lete in Paris; **144** The home of Nadia Yaron and Myriah Scruggs of Nightwood in Brooklyn; **145–146** The

Norfolk family home of the designer Petra Boase; **147** The home of James Russell & Hannah Plumb, the artists behind JamesPlumb www.jamesplumb.co.uk; **148l** www.dearswallow.com; **148–149** The restaurant 'Derrière' designed and owned by the 'Mazouz Brothers'; **150–151** The home of artist Claire Basler in France; **152** The home of Nadia Yaron and Myriah Scruggs of Nightwood in Brooklyn; **153** Home of Tim Rundle and Glynn Jones; **155in** www.aureliemathigot.com; **160** The French home of the interior stylist and consultant Sandrine Place.

business credits

Ann Shore
Creative
Story
The Old Truman Brewery
4–5 Dray Walk
off Brick Lane
London E1 6QL
T: +44 (0)20 7247 3137
Endpapers; 7 above right; 33 above left; 36; 60; 64–65; 86–87; 109; 120; 122–125; 134–135.

Aurelie Mathigot
Artist & designer
www.aureliemathigot.com
30 above left; 30 below right; 39 right; 42–43; 50; 58 above left; 58 centre; 58 below centre; 59; 75 above right; 82; 117; 137 below; 157 inset.

Cécile Daladier & Nicolas Soulier
Cecile Daladier: artist
Nicolas Soulier: architect
E: assai@free.fr
89; 90 below left; 105; 114–115.

Claire Basler
Artist
www.clairebasler.com
T: +33 6 75 87 31 38
3 inset; 4 inset; 7 above left; 8–9; 22; 48; 52; 54; 70 below right; 71; 73; 78; 94–95; 98–99; 106–107; 121; 130–131; 150–151.

David Alhadeff
The Future Perfect
(the original)
115 North 6ᵗʰ St.
Brooklyn
NY 11211
T:+ 00 1 718 599 6278

The Future Perfect (Manhattan)
55 Great Jones Street
NYC 10012
T: +00 1 212 473 2500
E: hello@thefutureperfect.com
www.thefutureperfect.com
51; 55 right; 57; 58 below right; 88 above; 116.

Dean Sawyer & Steve Drum
Interior architect & designer
E: Dean@jamesdeansawyer.com
www.jamesdeansawyer.com
5 centre; 40 above left; 47 below left; 58 below left; 80 inset; 90 above; 90 below right; 91, 101.

Deborah Bowness
Hand-printed wallpaper artist
www.deborahbowness.com
6, 10–11, 27, 50–51, 76–77.

Derrière
69 rue des Gravilliers
75003 Paris
T: +33 1 44 61 91 95
2; 7 below right; 26; 28 inset; 33 above right inset; 56 background; 58 above right; 69 below left; 72 below; 96; 103 below; 127; 148–149.

JamesPlumb
Work with the overlooked and discarded, taking time worn antiques and cast-offs to produce one-off assemblages, luminaries and interiors.
T: 020 7738 5547
www.jamesplumb.co.uk
us@jamesplumb.co.uk
7 below right; 23 below; 34 above right; 46; 67 left; 70 above right; 79; 97 left; 129; 147.

Kristin Norris & Trevor Lunn
Managing Director of
B H L D N & Executive
Creative Director of
Anthropologie
www.BHLDN.com
www.anthroplogie.com
5 above; 21; 34; 35; 55 left; 62 inset; 66 below; 81 inset; 83; 104; 119 above; 138 above.

Myriah Scruggs & Nadia Yaron
Nightwood
www.nightwoodny.com
5 below; 12; 15; 29 inset; 47 above left; 47 right; 53; 67 right; 112–113; 144; 152.

Nathalie Lete
Artist & designer
www.nathalie-lete.com
14 inset; 38 inset; 40 above right; 66 above; 68; 74; 75 above left; 131 right; 137 above; 138 below; 139; 142–143.

Nina Tolstrup
Designer
Studiomama
www.studiomama.com
24 right; 25; 72 above; 88 below; 119 below.

Petra Boase
Textile artist & designer
www.petraboase.com
www.cliffbarns.com
20; 30 above right; 40 below right; 41; 44–45; 56 above inset; 75 below; 92–93; 110–111; 136; 140–141; 145–146.

Ria Charisse
Jewellery designer & artist
www.dearswallow.com
33 below right; 34 below right; 63 inset; 69 above left; 69 above right; 69 centre; 70 left; 102; 103 above; 148 left.

Sandrine Place
Interior stylist and consultant
www.sandrineplace.com
23 above; 31; 34 above centre; 34 below left; 40 below left; 69 below right; 97 right; 108; 126 inset; 160.

Tim Rundle & Glynn Jones
www.suitcase-confessions.blogspot.com
1; 16–19; 24 above left; 24 below left; 30 below right; 32; 34 below centre; 56 below inset; 69 above centre; 84–85; 118; 132–133; 153.

index

acknowledgments

Firstly, a big, big thank you to Ryland Peters & Small for another, very, very special opportunity. In particular to Alison Starling for nurturing the initial idea, Leslie Harrington and Megan Smith for inspiring design and layout, Rebecca Woods for calmly organising copy, and Jess Walton for expertly putting plans into practice. Once again, thank you Ali Hanan for your endlessly up-beat approach and exceptionally inspiring way with words.

Finally, a huge and very special thank you to Debi Treloar, whose energy and curiosity never fails to inspire.

This book was a wonderful excuse to enter some amazingly inspiring homes. I would particularly like to thank: Tim Rundle, stylist and collector with an exceptional eye; Petra Boase, creative artist with a skill in inspirational home-making; James Russell and Hannah Plumb, talented designer duo known as JamesPlumb; Ann Shore, shop-owner and stylist with an unfailing visual signature; Nina Tolstrup, the colourful and creative individual behind Studiomama; Nathalie Lete, quirky, colourful and exceptional, illustrator, creator and friend; Aurelie Mathigot, fantastically talented textiles artist; Cécile Daladier and Nicolas Soulier, creatively combining architecture and botany; Claire Basler, artist extraordinaire; Sandrine Place, talented interior stylist and consultant; Kristin Norris, known for her unstoppable visually creative mind; Ria Charisse, designer of beautiful jewellery and environments; Nadia Yaron and Myriah Scruggs, skilled sustainable up-cyclers; David Alhadeff, creative shop-owner with an energetic eye and Dean Sawyer, inspirational interiors wizard!

Ali would like to thank Emily and Debi for their inspiration, constant creativity and friendship; she'd also like to give love and thanks to Dizzy, Luca and Rosa; and also a big thanks to her talented work partner, Diana Janicki, who inspires me daily.